This Indenture made the fourth day of October One thousand eight hundred and ninety ___ Between Thomas Gilbert Packham of Hall Place Harbledown in the County of Kent Esquire Charles Hill Devey of No 6 Mincing Lane in the City of London Esquire and Alexander Roberts of No 2 Conduit Street in the County of Middlesex Esquire of the first part Florence Mary Rogers of Westwood Cottage Church Road Richmond in the County of Surrey Widow of the second part William Brass of No 47 Old Street St Lukes in the County of Middlesex Contractor of the third part William Capel Slaughter and William May both of No 18 Austin Friars in the City of London Solicitor of the fourth part Richard Roberts of No 23 Laurence Pountney Lane in the City of London Architect of the fifth part and Sydney Elliott Preston of 18 Austin Friars aforesaid Solicitor of the sixth part

Whereas by an Indenture dated the twenty fourth day of April One thousand six hundred and ninety four therein expressed to be made between ____ and Young Sarah Barrington and Elizabeth Young of the one part and Robert Stamper of the other part Certain land within the precincts of the then late dissolved Monastery or Priory of St Austin otherwise Augustine Friars in the Parish of St Peter le Poor in the Ward of Broad Street London and upon which or parts of which then stood four messuages was demised to the said Robert Stamper his executors administrators and assigns thenceforth for the term of One thousand years Subject to a right of redemption by the said Richard Young afterwards ___ as hereinafter recited And whereas by an Indenture dated the twenty third day of April One thousand Seven hundred ... made between the said Robert Stamper and Richard Young of the one part and Daniel Baker of the other part the said hereditaments comprised in the said term were assigned to the said Daniel Baker his executors administrators and assigns for the residue of the same term subject to a right of redemption by the said Richard Young as therein mentioned And whereas by an Indenture dated the twenty ninth day of June One thousand seven hundred and two expressed to be made between the said Richard Young of the one part and Barbara Baker Widow Relict and Executrix of the last will and Testament of the said Daniel Baker then deceased of the other part the said Richard Young released unto the said Barbara Baker the equity or right of redemption then subsisting by virtue of the said Indenture of the twenty fourth day of April One thousand six hundred and ninety four and by the same Indenture the said Richard Young demised unto the said Barbara Baker her executors administrators and assigns a certain messuage in Austin Friars aforesaid with a piece of land adjoining on which a stable had been built To hold unto the said Barbara Baker her executors administrators and assigns thenceforth for the term of Five hundred years a right being to the said Richard Young to redeem the hereditaments comprised in the said terms of One thousand years and Five hundred years respectively on the payment of one thousand one hundred and eighty pounds but which right has long since become barred and extinguished And whereas after divers mesne assignments and operations of law ultimately by an Indenture dated the twenty third day of January One thousand eight hundred and sixty eight made between Benjamin Pleakes Gundry of the first part The London and County Land and Building Company Limited of the second part Pleakes Rex Gundry of the third part Thomas Alexander Roberts of the fourth part and the said Richard Roberts of the fifth part certain of the said hereditaments comprised in the Indenture last hereinbefore recited and including the hereditaments expressed to be hereby conveyed became vested in the said Thomas Alexander Roberts as to such part thereof as was comprised in the said terms respectively for the residue of the respective terms of One thousand years and Five hundred years ... created by the said two several Indentures of the twenty fourth April One thousand six hundred and ninety four and twenty ninth June One thousand seven hundred and two And by the same Indenture the fee simple of and in the hereditaments thereby conveyed as aforesaid expectant upon the determination of the said term was conveyed unto and to the use of the said Richard Roberts his heirs and assigns upon trust nevertheless for the said Thomas Alexander Roberts his heirs and assigns And whereas the said Thomas Alexander Roberts duly made his will dated the eighth day of August One thousand eight hundred and eighty seven and by ... inter alia gave and devised the hereditaments hereinafter described and expressed to be hereby conveyed by the description of "my freehold ... No 18 Austin Friars London" unto and to the use of his daughter the said Florence Mary Rogers her heirs executors administrators and assigns for her sole and separate use absolutely And whereas the said Thomas Alexander Roberts died on the sixth day of October One thousand eight hundred and eighty eight without having revoked or altered his said will which was duly proved on the tenth day of December One thousand eight hundred and eighty eight in the Principal Registry of the Probate Division of Her Majesty's High Court of Justice by Roberts the Executors therein named And whereas the said Florence Mary Rogers lately contracted with the said William Brass for the ... hereby conveyed thereof has yet been executed to the said William Brass And whereas the said William May to transfer to them the benefit of the said Contract upon the terms of the said William Capel Slaughter and William May paying to him the said sum of Twenty one thousand pounds agreed to be paid by the said William Brass for the purchase of the said premises as aforesaid the ... of the property comprised in the term of Five hundred years from the term comprised in the term of Five hundred years cannot now be ... hereditaments expressed to be hereby conveyed or any part thereof is included And whereas the parties hereto of the first and second parts respectively

Now this Indenture witnesseth that in pursuance of the said agreements and in consideration of the sum of Twenty one thousand pounds paid to the said William Brass respectively paid by the said William Capel Slaughter and William May (the receipt of which respective sums they the said Thomas Gilbert Packham Charles Hill Devey and Alexander Roberts as such personal representatives as aforesaid and by the ... heirs as beneficial Owner at the request of the said William Brass doth hereby convey and confirm and the said William Brass as ... hereby confirms unto the ... situated on the West side of Austin Friars in the parish of St Peter the Poor in the City of London upon which stands a messuage or tenement known as No 18 Austin ... are delineated in the plan drawn on these Presents and are therein colored purple it being however ... declared that no further rights over the portion marked ... of the twenty third January One thousand eight hundred and sixty eight are intended to be hereby conveyed To Hold the same subject to existing tenancies administrators and assigns as joint tenants as to the part thereof comprised in the said term of One thousand years created by the said Indenture of the twenty fourth ... of the said term and as to the remaining part thereof for the residue unexpired of the term of Five hundred years created by the said Indenture of the twenty ninth April One thousand eight hundred and sixty eight ... witnesseth that in pursuance of the said agreements and for the considerations aforesaid the said Richard Roberts as trustee by the direction of the said Florence Mary Rogers as Beneficial Owner hereby conveys and confirms and the said William Brass as ... hereby confirms unto the said Sydney Elliott ... to be hereby conveyed To Hold unto and to the use of the said Sydney Elliott Preston his heirs and assigns in fee simple subject to the said terms of years in so far as now ... and William Capel Slaughter and William May their heirs and assigns as joint tenants And the said Florence Mary Rogers doth hereby acknowledge the right ... hereinbefore recited Indenture of the twenty third January One thousand eight hundred and sixty eight and to delivery of copies thereof and hereby undertakes for the safe custody ... set their hands and seals the day and year first above written

Florence M. Rogers. —

___ Brass.

___ Slaughter

___ May

Richard Roberts

Sydney Elliott ___ Preston

SLAUGHTER AND MAY

A SHORT HISTORY

SLAUGHTER AND MAY

A SHORT HISTORY

LAURIE DENNETT

Granta Editions

© Slaughter and May 1989

ISBN 0 906782 42 2

Published by
Granta Editions
47 Norfolk Street
Cambridge CB1 2LE
Granta Editions is an imprint of The Book Concern Ltd

Designed by Kate Mott
Design and production in association with
Book Production Consultants, 47 Norfolk Street, Cambridge

Typeset by Cambridge Photosetting Services
Printed and bound by Butler & Tanner, Frome, Somerset

Contents

Illustrations

LIST OF ILLUSTRATIONS

Foreword

The last 100 years have been a period of rapid change, particularly in the City, and yet in some ways little has changed. In 1889 when William Slaughter and William May set up in partnership in Austin Friars they had none of the communications and other equipment we now take for granted – photocopiers, word processors, computers and fax machines – and telephones were only just starting to come into use.

They did however have the ability to provide not only technical excellence but sound and constructive advice and they saw the importance of understanding the needs of their clients.

A century later the practice continues to be based on these principles and in those terms nothing has changed except the speed of response aided by technological developments over recent years.

The Firm was an immediate success when it first opened its doors in 1889 and its continuing success is due both to the soundness of the foundations laid by William Slaughter and William May and to the qualities and efforts of succeeding generations of partners and members of staff.

The Firm has played a substantial role in the development of the City over the last 100 years. The surge of business in the City and the plethora of regulations affecting its operations are likely to increase the need for legal advice of the highest quality in the future. Slaughter and May looks forward to its next 100 years.

George Inglis

January 1989

Author's Preface

Writing the history of Slaughter and May has been an honour and a pleasure, and the acknowledgement of the contributions made by others is equally so. Foremost among those to whom my thanks are due are Adrian Smart, Peter Morley-Jacob and Peter Langley of Slaughter and May, and Stephanie Zarach and Professor Theo Barker of Debrett's Business History Research, who organised the practical aspects of the project and assisted in the production of the manuscript in a multitude of ways. While I have benefited from the advice and assistance of many people at Slaughter and May (past and present), I would particularly like to thank the three partners mentioned above for their unstinting help in following up specific points of research, Nicholas Heroys for his analysis of some financial records and John Remnant for exceptionally painstaking and skilled genealogical research on the Slaughter, May and Capel families. To three former senior partners I owe special thanks: to Christopher Clarke,

for his kindness in applying his remarkable memory to the countless questions put to him; to Peter Marriage for some challenging photographic work; and to Tony Mallinson for advice on the modern period.

A number of individuals have loaned historic material or provided photographs. In this connection I would especially like to thank Robert May, Anthony Drewe and Rodolphe d'Erlanger. For the detailed study of *Burdett's Official Intelligence* I would like to thank Meta Zimmeck. Simon Combe, Mark Lello, Adam Levin, Moz Scott, Jane Hands, Elizabeth Thomas and Sara Vaughan were kind enough to help in listing a large quantity of previously unsorted records. Edward Keeble generously executed drawings to order and at short notice. Typing throughout has been done by Sally Hunt and Pauline Hurring. I am also grateful to Pauline Hurring for practical assistance in the final stages of the project.

Slaughter and May is unusual among

the City's leading partnerships in not having lost its records during the last war. None the less, many records were destroyed before the move from Austin Friars to Basinghall Street in 1968, and this has resulted, inevitably, in some gaps. The astonishing amount of information that has been discovered on the earliest years of the partnership has been some recompense for gaps later on. Foremost among the sources that came to light in writing the history of Slaughter and May were William May's diaries and William Slaughter's correspondence with Julius Drewe on the subject of the Home and Colonial Stores, which brought the founders of the firm to life in a way no other material had. The stamp of their personalities is still evident in the character of the firm today, in the exceptionally high standards and imaginative outlook it maintains.

Laurie Dennett
London
January 1989

CHAPTER 1

In which William Slaughter and William May enter into Partnership

On the morning of Tuesday, 1st January 1889, two young solicitors, William Capel Slaughter and William May, paid a visit to the office of the Consolidated Bank in Threadneedle Street in the City of London. Although it was 1st January, it was an ordinary working day in the City; New Year's Day was not to become a public holiday for another 85

The signatures of William Slaughter and William May in the Register of Consolidated Bank Limited, Threadneedle Street. 1st January 1889 was the date on which the two men opened a joint bank account and formally established their partnership.

years. For William Slaughter and William May, it was something more than a working day or even the first day of the new year. When they signed the huge registry book at the bank (now National Westminster Bank) to open an account in their joint names, they formalised the working arrangement that had existed between them for the previous 12 months, and established the partnership of Slaughter and May.

One hundred years later, Slaughter and May has 77 partners and an international practice that employs over 1,000 staff

worldwide. The City has changed out of all recognition in that time. Apart from the cartoons of the founders and a watercolour of the firm's original premises that decorate the walls of the partners' luncheon room at 35 Basinghall Street, there is outwardly little to remind anyone in Slaughter and May today of its birth a century ago. Yet tangible, if invisible, links survive. The firm had its bank account at the same Threadneedle Street branch until the latter closed in 1988. In the year of its centenary the partnership still acts for some of its earliest clients. There are also the snippets of corporate lore that proliferate in any firm, passed from partner to articled clerk down the decades. In the case of Slaughter and May, some of these impressions have proved to be remarkably close to the facts as borne out by other evidence. Everyone from the partners down, for instance, 'knows' that the founders met while both were in the employ of the firm of Ashurst Morris Crisp & Co., and that they set up together because there was no likelihood of partnerships there. But this is only half the story. How many know of the extraordinary business agreement between William Slaughter and his former employer that got the new partnership off to a flying start? (All memory of it had been lost, and until some assiduous digging unearthed a revealing correspondence, its existence was unsuspected.) Other often repeated stories have been shown to possess no

William Capel Slaughter (11th May 1857–10th March 1917), depicted as 'CITY LAW' in Mayfair and Town Topics, *April 1911.*

truth at all. The most frequently repeated tag, and, as it emerged, the least justified by the evidence, is the one asserting that William Slaughter provided 'the brains' of the partnership, and William May 'the money'. How many people in the firm today know that Slaughter's own wealth was not inconsiderable, or that May, far from lacking the intellect and energy of his partner, composed and published music, planted his foot atop Mont Blanc and the Matterhorn, and was widely regarded in the City as one of the leading corporate lawyers of his day?

All this is merely to emphasise, if it needs emphasising, that the stuff of history is, more often than not, more interesting than fiction. Far from replacing colourful corporate legends by documented realities that are distinctly less compelling, the wealth of information that has come to light in the course of charting the partnership's history has in almost every instance eclipsed the hand-me-down accounts. To mark the occasion of Slaughter and May's 100th anniversary, it seemed fitting that the fictions – or semi-fictions – should be replaced by more substantial narratives. The present version, concise and light in tone, is intended for a wide readership. For the legal and City communities of which Slaughter and May has been a part for 100 years, and which may have an interest in the partnership's history for the light it sheds upon their own, a fuller version of the history has also been prepared.

William May (4th May 1863–6th May 1932), depicted as 'LAW', date and publication unknown.

From 1889 to 1900, the firm of Slaughter and May consisted solely of its two founders and the few clerks and staff that they employed. Despite a professional association and a friendship that lasted all their lives, the backgrounds of the partners were very different. Slaughter was the elder by six years; he was 31 to May's 25 when they joined forces, and consequently had the greater legal experience. He was also the initiator of the partnership. Both men's origins and connections, but particularly Slaughter's, were important factors in the early success of the firm.

Slaughter was born on 11th May 1857, the sixth and youngest child and second son of Mihill Slaughter, Secretary of the Railway Department of The Stock Exchange, and Ann Erskine Capel Slaughter. Many members of his mother's family, the Capels, were independent tradesmen, but

Broxup Z. Wholefale Perfumer, 138, Oxford-ftreet
Bruce Rich. Infurance broker, 5, Bartholomew-lane
Brucker Geo. & Son, Sugar-refiners, 1, Little Diftaff-lane
Bruckfhaw & Capel, Stock-brokers, 96, Cornhill
Brumfield & Slack, Gold & Silver Lacemen, 6, Lawrence-la.
Bruniges Martin, Sugar-refiner, Wentworth-ftreet, Spitalfields
Brunnell Tho. Silk Weaver, 83, Cow-crofs-ftreet, Smithfield
BrunfdonC. Blackwelhall factor&Warehoufeman,70,Bafinghall-ft.

A trade directory entry for the year 1796, showing the stockbroking partnership of Bruckshaw & Capel (later Capel Cuertons & Cundy) in which William Slaughter's great-uncle, John Capel, was a partner.

the comparative wealth and higher social standing of three of her immediate relatives derived from finance. Her father, James Durnford Capel, was a cashier of the Bank of England from 1793 to 1844. John Capel, his brother, was a broker and partner of Bruckshaw & Capel (later Capel Cuertons & Cundy) and a member of the Committee for General Purposes of The Stock Exchange. James Capel, a cousin of John and James Durnford, began as a stockbroker in John's firm, but became a partner in the one which eventually became James Capel & Co. Both this James and his cousin John were Trustees and Managers of The Stock Exchange for long periods of their careers, and James in addition served as chairman of its Benevolent Fund for 44 years.

Slark William, *Tinman*, 10, Cheapfide
Slater, Hanrott & Burkett, *Chemifts & Druggifts*, 7, Poultry
Slater Thomas, *Warehoufeman*, 65, Bafinghall-ftreet
Slater Thomas, *Tea-dealer & Grocer*, 54, Fore-ftr. Moorfields
Slaughter William and Edmund, *Cheefemongers*, 5, Bearbinder-lane
Sice John, *Wine Merchant*, 96, Borough High-ftreet
Slipper & Allanfon, *Man's-mercers*, 6, New-ftr. Covent-garden
Sloman John and John and T. Picard, *Linen-drapers*, 1, Friday-ftreet, Cheapfide

William Slaughter (1743–1818), the great-grandfather of the William Capel Slaughter of Slaughter and May, was a cheesemonger, first at 5 Bearbinder Lane in the City and, from 1788, at 114 St Martin's Lane just off Trafalgar Square. William's son Mihill (1781–1817) died young, leaving five children to be brought up by relatives. Fortunately the family was already prosperous.

On his father's side, William Capel Slaughter could trace his descent from another William Slaughter, a cheesemonger, whose shop at 114 St Martin's Lane, from 1788 onwards, was coincidentally the same shop that a member of the Capel family had previously owned. William Slaughter the elder and his wife Mary Mihill were the great-grandparents of William Capel Slaughter. Their elder son Mihill, who shared the cheese business, died at the age of 36 in 1817, leaving five children, the eldest of whom was also called Mihill. It was this Mihill – the father of William Capel Slaughter – who in

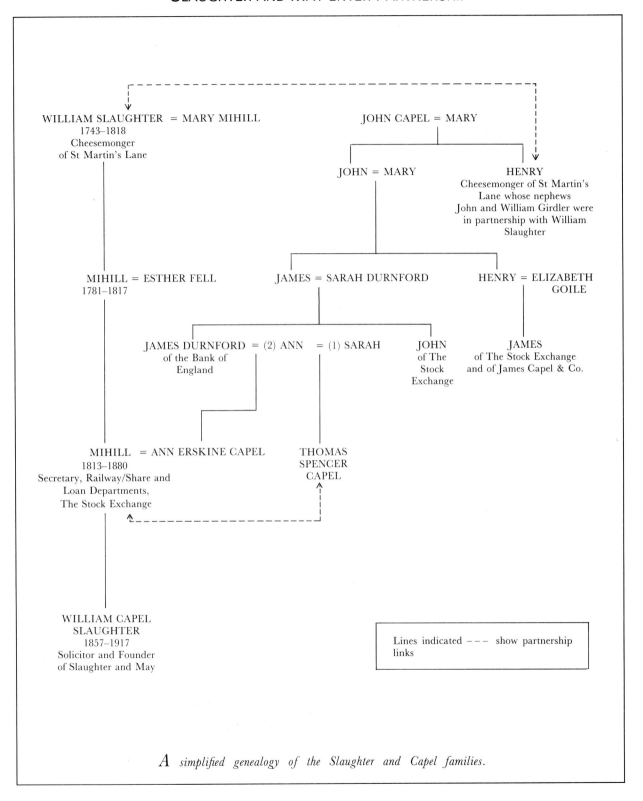

WILLIAM SLAUGHTER = MARY MIHILL
1743–1818
Cheesemonger
of St Martin's Lane

JOHN CAPEL = MARY

JOHN = MARY

HENRY
Cheesemonger of St Martin's
Lane whose nephews
John and William Girdler were
in partnership with William
Slaughter

MIHILL = ESTHER FELL
1781–1817

JAMES = SARAH DURNFORD

HENRY = ELIZABETH
GOILE

JAMES DURNFORD = (2) ANN = (1) SARAH
of the Bank of
England

JOHN
of The
Stock
Exchange

JAMES
of The Stock Exchange
and of James Capel & Co.

MIHILL = ANN ERSKINE CAPEL
1813–1880
Secretary, Railway/Share and
Loan Departments,
The Stock Exchange

THOMAS
SPENCER
CAPEL

WILLIAM CAPEL
SLAUGHTER
1857–1917
Solicitor and Founder
of Slaughter and May

Lines indicated – – – show partnership
links

A simplified genealogy of the Slaughter and Capel families.

Capel Henry & Co. wine merchants, 17 Lit. Tower street
Capel Henry&Co. coopers, 17 Lit. Tower st. & 14 Seething la
Capel(Jas.)Norbury&Trotter,stockbrokers,5 Throgmorton st
Capel & Slaughter, coal merchants, Bridewell wharf, Bride-
  well precinct, William street, Blackfriars
Capel Henry, wine merchant, 4 Cooper's row, Crutched friars
Capel Thomas, grocer, 9 North st. Manchester square

A trade directory entry for the year 1842, showing the coal-merchants' business of Capel & Slaughter, in which William Capel Slaughter's father, Mihill, was a partner.

1835 went into partnership as a coal mer-chant at Bridewell Wharf, Blackfriars, with one Thomas Spencer Capel (under the name of Capel & Slaughter) and who, in 1846 married his partner's half-sister, Ann Erskine Capel. At about the same time, he changed his occupation, almost certainly with the help of James Capel, Ann's first cousin once removed.

The mid-1840s were the years of the 'railway mania' which, following an earlier boom and then a somewhat slack period for railway shares, saw a tremendous growth in railway investment. Between 1843 and 1850, the total paid-up railway share capital increased from £43 million to £187 million. This surge of activity had important effects on The Stock Exchange. It created the only market outside the existing one for Government securities and paved the way for a similar market in company shares. James Capel's firm was heavily involved in railway share dealing. Capel was in a position to appreciate the need for a railways' department within The Stock Exchange and, as a member of many of the Exchange's committees, to influence the choice of Secretary. Mihill Slaughter was appointed to the newly created post and held it until the Railways' Department was absorbed into the Share and Loan Department in 1863, whereupon

Mihill Slaughter (1813–1880) the father of William Capel Slaughter and Secretary, first of the Railways' Department, then of the Share and Loan Department of The Stock Exchange, from the mid-1840s to his death in 1880.

he was made Secretary of that department and remained so until his death in 1880.

One of the job's most important duties was to provide brokers and clients with sufficient information to enable them to distinguish, among a host of promotions, the potentially successful from the poten-tially disastrous. For the whole of his career, Mihill Slaughter compiled and edited a publication that was invaluable to anyone connected with the market. It first appeared in 1849 and thereafter was pub-lished half-yearly under the authority of the Committee of The Stock Exchange under the title *Railway Intelligence*. This publication, the forerunner of *The Stock Exchange Official Yearbook*, was based on a lengthy questionnaire devised by Mihill and sent out to hundreds of railway companies. The replies were broken down and tabulated to provide a compendium of information on railway companies and systems, railway statistics, and the securities issued by British and foreign railway interests. The first few volumes were slender, but by 1860 each contained over 300 pages.

The post of Secretary was both responsible and lucrative; it carried a salary and also an attractive perquisite, in the form of an exclusive right to sell documentary stamps to members of The Stock Exchange under licence from the Inland Revenue. Stamp Duty was paid on the consideration passing on each transaction, and the commission earned together with

CAPEL COURT.—RAILWAY SPECULATORS.

At the height of the 'railway mania' of the mid-1840s speculators carried on a market outside The Stock Exchange.

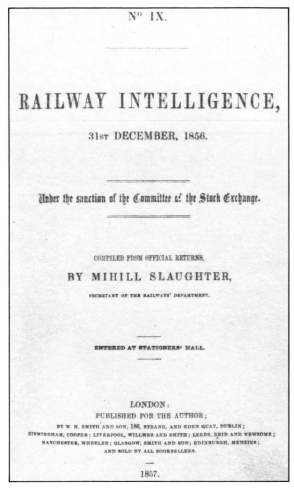

Nᵒ IX.

RAILWAY INTELLIGENCE,

31st DECEMBER, 1856.

Under the sanction of the Committee of the Stock Exchange.

COMPILED FROM OFFICIAL RETURNS,

BY MIHILL SLAUGHTER,

SECRETARY OF THE RAILWAYS' DEPARTMENT.

ENTERED AT STATIONERS' HALL.

LONDON:
PUBLISHED FOR THE AUTHOR;
BY W. H. SMITH AND SON, 186, STRAND, AND EDEN QUAY, DUBLIN;
BIRMINGHAM, COOPER ; LIVERPOOL, WILLMER AND SMITH ; LEEDS, REID AND NEWSOME ;
MANCHESTER, WHEELER ; GLASGOW, SMITH AND SON ; EDINBURGH, MENZIES ;
AND SOLD BY ALL BOOKSELLERS.

1857.

Title page from Railway Intelligence, *1857 edition. This publication was an invaluable aid to the investor in railway shares and was the forerunner of today's Stock Exchange Official Yearbook. The information it contained was compiled from questionnaires devised by Mihill Slaughter.*

his salary and fairly substantial family inheritances brought Mihill Slaughter and his family a comfortable standard of living. Shortly after the birth of their first son, another Mihill, in 1847, the Slaughters moved to the fashionable suburb of Brixton, newly accessible to the City by horse-drawn omnibus. Four daughters

were born between 1850 and 1856, and finally, ten years after his brother, William Capel Slaughter was born in 1857.

Little information survives about William Slaughter's upbringing. He was privately educated and did not attend university. Instead he decided to train as a solicitor. A university education was still an exceptional qualification in a young man entering articles, despite the higher educational standards demanded by the profession in the 20 years following the gradual introduction of the reforms in legal education recommended by a Select Committee in 1846. The firm where Slaughter spent five years in articles (as opposed to the three permitted to graduates) was the partnership of Benjamin Gay Wilkinson and George Bernard Harvey Drew, in Bermondsey Street, Southwark. Slaughter was articled to Wilkinson, the senior partner. The practice dated from the middle of the eighteenth century, and derived much of its work from clerical and local authority connections as well as from private clients. One important area where it seems not to have been active was commercial law, the field in which Slaughter was later to specialise.

With his father still active at The Stock Exchange and his elder brother Mihill by now a stockjobber, Slaughter may have discovered where his own interests lay in the contrast between the commercial concerns discussed at home and the work he did at Wilkinson and Drew. Probably because of his father's wide acquaintance, William's lack of commercial experience proved no barrier to joining a City law practice when he qualified as a solicitor in July 1879. It was more than likely by way

No.	When and where born	Name, if any	Sex	Name and surname of father	Name, surname and maiden surname of mother	Occupation of father	Signature, description and residence of informant	When registered	Signature of registrar
98	Eleventh May 1857 9 Langton Place	William Capel	Boy	Mehill Slaughter	Ann Erskine Slaughter formerly Capel	Member Stock Exchange	Ann C. Slaughter Mother 9 Langton Place Vassall Road	Ninth June 1857	The Wm Boult Registrar

*B*irth certificate of William Capel Slaughter, 11th May 1857. Slaughter's birthplace, 9 Langton Place, Vassall Road, Kennington, no longer exists.

of his father's introduction that he was appointed an assistant solicitor in one of the City's leading commercial practices, Ashurst Morris Crisp & Co. of 6 Old Jewry.

Ashurst Morris Crisp was distinguished from the run of City law firms by several features, not the least of which were the talents of two of its partners, John Morris and Frank (later Sir Frank) Crisp. The radical politics of its founder, William Henry Ashurst (1792–1855) and his son of the same name (1819–1879) had set it apart long before Morris or Crisp ever became partners. The Ashursts, father and son and their families, were among the nineteenth century's most vocal and effective reformers. They supported, both financially and morally, almost every progressive cause from the 1832 Reform Bill onwards, including anti-slavery, Chartism, postal reform, poor relief, feminism, the peace movement in Britain and the nationalist movements that arose in countries such as Italy and Hungary after 1848. But if the Ashursts' political opinions distinguished the firm, so too did its close association with the mercantile and financial empire of the entrepreneur James Morrison, whose vast Fore Street Warehouse earned him the popular title of

the 'Napoleon of Shopkeepers', and who on his death in 1854 left a personal fortune second in extent only to Nathan Rothschild's. The connection with Morrison, who shared the Ashursts' political views, dated from 1823, but the law firm benefited from the investments made by Morrison and his sons over the next several decades in the United States and South America, mainly in railways.

John Morris, the senior partner at the time William Slaughter joined Ashurst

*J*ohn Morris, one of the City's foremost solicitors from the 1860s until his death in 1905, and mentor of William Capel Slaughter. Morris entered the firm of Ashurst Morris Crisp as a clerk, completed six years' articles and was made a partner in 1854. He became senior partner in 1862.

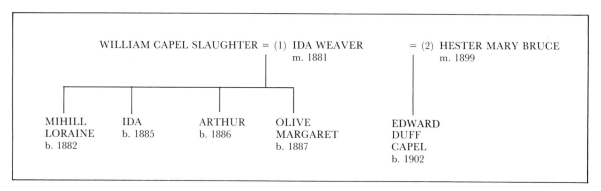

```
WILLIAM CAPEL SLAUGHTER = (1)  IDA WEAVER          = (2)  HESTER MARY BRUCE
                               m. 1881                   m. 1899


MIHILL          IDA         ARTHUR        OLIVE            EDWARD
LORAINE         b. 1885     b. 1886       MARGARET         DUFF
b. 1882                                   b. 1887          CAPEL
                                                           b. 1902
```

This much simplified chart shows William Capel Slaughter's two marriages and his children by each.

Morris Crisp, had gained his legal experience in dealing with the Morrison interests. As a result of major schemes of arrangement he devised for companies in which the Morrisons were involved, he was an acknowledged authority on company reconstructions and his expert help was called upon in the aftermath of the crash of a major bank, Overend Gurney, in 1866, and numerous other crashes and liquidations. Morris drafted the main provisions of the Joint Stock Companies Arrangement Act of 1870, which provided that where a company was in liquidation, a scheme of arrangement approved by 75 per cent in value of its creditors and sanctioned by the Court should be binding on all the creditors. Previously a unanimous vote had been required. Morris's concern to put a failed company back on its feet for the benefit of all the creditors, not just the

secured few, was typical of his positive approach to business.

This approach was exactly right for the economic climate of the 1880s. The economy was expanding again after the bad slump of the late 1870s, one of the worst of the century. New opportunities to develop railways and natural resources abroad and utilities and manufacturing at home, brought Ashurst Morris Crisp vast amounts of legal work. It was in this energetic atmosphere that William Slaughter spent the first decade of his professional life. By now too his personal life was becoming more settled. His father, Mihill Slaughter the elder, died in 1880 after more than 30 years at The Stock Exchange, leaving an estate worth £40,000 – over £1 million at today's values – so that William and the rest of the family were well provided for. In September 1881 he married Ida Mabel Weaver, the daughter of a surgeon, who bore him four children between 1882 and 1887 (one of whom died

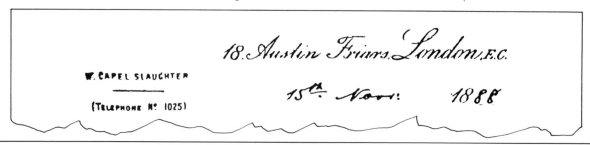

18. Austin Friars, London, E.C.

W. CAPEL SLAUGHTER

(TELEPHONE Nº 1025)

15ᵗʰ Novᵣ: 1888

as a baby) but of whom little is otherwise known. On their marriage, William and Ida drew up the kind of financial settlement common at the time. One of its clauses obliged the trustees to raise, from the funds Slaughter contributed, the sum of £5,000 to buy him a partnership or set him up in independent practice whenever he decided to take this step. This was a considerable sum for a young man to have at his disposal – worth something like £150,000 at today's values – and it by no means accounted for all of Slaughter's wealth. Even without taking his earnings into account, he was a well-to-do young man.

Ashurst Morris Crisp, like most partnerships of the period, had a very small number of partners. In the mid-1890s, three men – John Morris, his nephew William Ashurst Morris, and Frank Crisp – handled the legal affairs of more than 300 companies, a high proportion of which were involved in railways, utilities, or exploring, mining or land ventures in the British colonies or the Americas. William Slaughter began by working alongside Morris, but within a few years was assuming complete responsibility for the legal affairs of some clients. In promoting companies in which those clients were involved, Slaughter attended to all the necessary arrangements, gaining valuable experience of the market-place. Some of his clients, such as Baron Emile d'Erlanger, were among the firm's most influential.

The degree of independence Slaughter achieved was unusual for an assistant solicitor and indicates that the partners must have had a high opinion of his

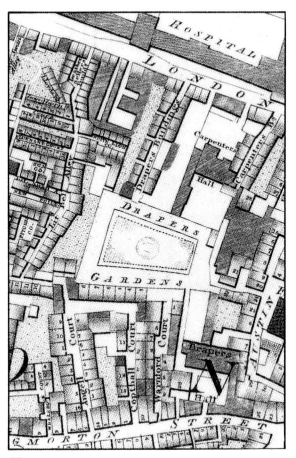

This map shows the west side of Austin Friars, Drapers Gardens, and the eventual site of Throgmorton Avenue. The area covered by Number 18 Austin Friars from 1892 onwards is roughly that of Numbers '6', '7' and '8' (actually '16', '17' and '18', as the preliminary '1's have been left off) facing the small cul-de-sac at the top of Austin Friars.

ability. Some time in 1887, he set up an office at 18 Austin Friars, a block of offices backing on to the new building being put up by John Morris at 9–17 Throgmorton Avenue to replace the headquarters at 6 Old Jewry, a crowded warren that his firm had occupied since 1846.

Slaughter's status once he had moved from Old Jewry is not easy to define. On one hand the admission of John Morris's youngest son, Edward Ashurst Morris, to the partnership in 1887 may have been a factor in Slaughter's departure. Both Morris and Slaughter may have felt, since there was no likelihood that further partners would be appointed in the near future, that it was in Slaughter's best interests to set up on his own.

On the other hand, it is evident that Slaughter was a valued associate. What appears to have occurred was that Slaughter became legally independent in 1887, having set up his own practice, but continued to act for certain clients as agent of Ashurst Morris Crisp.

Not only was this an amicable arrangement, but it was designed by Morris to help Slaughter establish himself rapidly and securely. Of those clients whose affairs Slaughter handled, some were from now on to be dealt with by him in his own name, and others by him as agent for Ashurst Morris Crisp, and in that firm's name. Morris made it clear to clients, in correspondence which survives, that he fully endorsed the arrangement. He also emphasised to them that the authority and experience of his firm would continue to be available to them, just as it was when Slaughter worked under the same roof and on the same basis as the rest of the firm.

The timing of this arrangement is confirmed by the evidence of another source, the diary for the year 1887 kept by the young William May, then nearing the end of his three year term of articles at Ashurst Morris Crisp. Not unnaturally, May was concerned about his own prospects after his admission now that there were four partners in the firm. May's diary gives no clues as to whether he and Slaughter were already on friendly terms. It relates only that the two on several occasions discussed May's future in the firm as an assistant solicitor after qualifying, and from the entries it is evident that May did not rate his chances of advancement very highly. In December 1887, just before Christmas, he recorded that he had had 'a long talk with Slaughter as to going with him next year'.

At this point, as well as dealing with the affairs of his clients, Slaughter was much concerned with the reconstruction of the Home and Colonial Trading Association, largely owned by Julius Drew, whose brother had married Slaughter's sister Elizabeth in 1882. He may have been particularly in need of an assistant – John Morris may even have suggested May as a suitable one, knowing, as in Slaughter's case, that the situation at Ashurst Morris Crisp was unlikely to change. For his part, May considered the idea over the Christmas break, and finally wrote to Slaughter on 31st December to accept. Although May sat his examinations in January 1888 and was admitted in the following July, it is likely, since 'William May, Gentleman, of 18 Austin Friars' was a signatory to the Home and Colonial Memorandum of Association of March 1888, that he moved into Slaughter's offices as soon as his examinations were over.

Slaughter could not have chosen as his assistant a young man whose background was more different from his own. May was a product of a land-owning family which could trace its ancestry back to the sixteenth century in the same part of

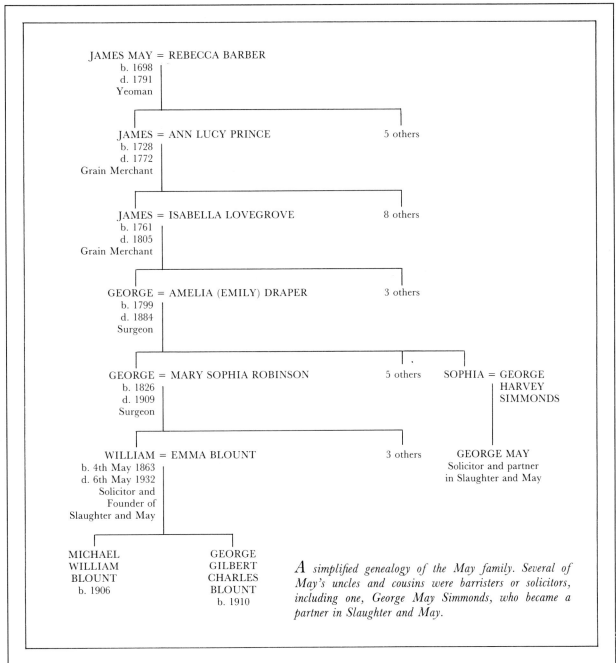

JAMES MAY = REBECCA BARBER
b. 1698
d. 1791
Yeoman

JAMES = ANN LUCY PRINCE   5 others
b. 1728
d. 1772
Grain Merchant

JAMES = ISABELLA LOVEGROVE   8 others
b. 1761
d. 1805
Grain Merchant

GEORGE = AMELIA (EMILY) DRAPER   3 others
b. 1799
d. 1884
Surgeon

GEORGE = MARY SOPHIA ROBINSON   5 others   SOPHIA = GEORGE
b. 1826   HARVEY
d. 1909   SIMMONDS
Surgeon

WILLIAM = EMMA BLOUNT   3 others   GEORGE MAY
b. 4th May 1863   Solicitor and partner
d. 6th May 1932   in Slaughter and May
Solicitor and
Founder of
Slaughter and May

MICHAEL   GEORGE
WILLIAM   GILBERT
BLOUNT   CHARLES
b. 1906   BLOUNT
                 b. 1910

A simplified genealogy of the May family. Several of May's uncles and cousins were barristers or solicitors, including one, George May Simmonds, who became a partner in Slaughter and May.

the Thames Valley, but which in recent generations had sent many members into the professions. Both his father and grandfather were eminent surgeons. His grandfather, George May senior, was a founder member of the British Medical Association, and both he and his son of the same name served as surgeons to the Royal Berkshire Hospital. Among William May's close relatives there were several

William May as a young man at Oxford.

law exams, January 1888, suggests that he entered Ashurst Morris Crisp early in 1885. It is possible that his school friendship with Edward Ashurst Morris influenced his choice of firm.

The impression of May that emerges from his diaries is not that of a man who could have followed his father and grandfather into medicine. May's interests were literary and artistic, rather than scientific, and his initial choice of the law probably owed something to family precedent. As a young man he read profusely and produced reams of verse. He was also musically gifted, playing the piano and cello well, and studying the latter at the Guildhall School in the evenings during his articles. Four of his musical compositions were later published. Apart from these interests, he retained a great love of the outdoors and open-air pursuits such as sailing, shooting, climbing and riding, and games like tennis and cricket. Though he was genuinely absorbed by the law and found the City a stimulating environment, he needed the counterbalance of country quiet and space to be at rights with the world. In this he differed from William Slaughter, whose chief satisfaction derived from his work. For Slaughter the working day had no end; his life revolved around his clients and their projects.

The temperamental differences between the two men proved to be more complementary than divisive. Before the end of 1888 they had decided to go into partnership. If either party gained more by this than the other, it was probably May, who at 25 and newly qualified, acquired at once an independence and a status that might otherwise have taken far longer to achieve.

barristers and solicitors to leaven the strong landowning and farming interest. William May was born on 4th May 1863, the eldest of George May junior's four children. His father and grandfather were at that time both practising at Reading, and May grew up in a vast house, The Warren, fronting the Thames at Caversham. In 1876 he was sent to Charterhouse, where he almost certainly encountered John Morris's son, Edward Ashurst Morris, who had entered the same house in the same quarter. May was an excellent scholar, and went on to Oxford where he read classics and modern history. He stayed on for an extra term to take a course in religious studies and took his degree in December 1884. The date of his

Four of William May's musical compositions were published in his lifetime.

A M C ^o & Slaughter 2/1/00

Matters in initialled List and any others handed over, or as to which Mr Slaughter's assistance may be — required, either altogether or partially, tobe conducted by Slaughter as follows :—

(a) Those conducted in our name as our Agent.

(b) Those in his own name on his own behalf.

We to allow him 2/3^{rds} of his — charges and one half of Special fees under "**a**" and he to allow us one third of his ordinary charges (ex- disbursement items) and one half of all special fees under "b" — Mr Morris to decide as to such ranking in case of difference.

The above to apply also to all matters growing out of those above referred to either "a" or "b". Mr Morris in like manner to decide thereon in case of difference.

Wm Capel Slaughter

On 2nd January 1888 John Morris and William Slaughter formulated the agreement under which William Slaughter was to continue to act for certain clients of Ashurst Morris Crisp. It was this agreement, renewed a year later, which gave the Slaughter and May partnership an excellent start.

CHAPTER 2

. . . *And establish themselves in the City*

There can be few law firms that have commenced practice on such a sound footing as did Slaughter and May. Thanks to John Morris's generosity and Slaughter's ability, the new partnership had a ready-made list of clients. One of Slaughter's first tasks on the formation of Slaughter and May was, at Morris's suggestion, to renew the agreement between them, principally to clarify the question of fee-sharing. In a proposal dated 2nd January 1888, Morris had listed two sets of clients: 25 for which Slaughter acted on behalf of Ashurst Morris Crisp, and six for which he acted in his own name. On the formation of Slaughter and May, the two men agreed that the partners should have two thirds of their charges and one half of special fees, but over the next few weeks this was amended so that they received one third of their charges to cover expenses, with the remainder to be divided equally between the two partnerships.

This agreement, once finalised in April 1889, lasted at least until John Morris's death in 1905, and possibly longer. Whether it has a counterpart in the origin of any other firm is impossible to say; but if not unique, it is surely very unusual and reflects the particular understanding that existed between Morris and Slaughter, as mentor and protégé. If Slaughter and May benefited from the formal agreement with John Morris, this did not mean any lessening of informal links. Where Morris was chairman or director of a company (as he was of the River Plate Trust Loan and Agency Company which administered the Morrison interests in South America), he sometimes offered work to Slaughter and May to avoid the conflict of interest that could have arisen had it gone to his own firm.

The most important of the clients to make the transition from Ashurst Morris Crisp to Slaughter and May was, without doubt, Baron Emile d'Erlanger, for two of whose companies, based in the United States, Slaughter had for some time already been acting. Most of the African and South American and much of the mining and railway business that came to Slaughter and May during its first 20 years came by way of Emile Erlanger and Company. It was through Baron d'Erlanger too, that Slaughter and May was introduced to other banks, such as J Henry Schroder and Company, and to individuals, such as the railway contractor George Pauling, who also became clients and in their turn brought the firm additional introductions.

Baron Emile d'Erlanger the elder (1832–1911) who was one of Slaughter and May's earliest and most influential clients. The association with Emile Erlanger & Co was to be very important, particularly in the years up to 1914.

Business lunch, by an unknown artist, showing among others Baron Emile d'Erlanger the younger and William Slaughter.

There was one client which, though it did not bring in others, none the less generated a vast amount of work of its own. This was Home and Colonial Stores, in whose organisation and expansion Slaughter had been deeply involved since its birth as The Home and Colonial Trading Association. Slaughter's sister's brother-in-law, Julius Drew, a Liverpool-based tea dealer with family links to the tea trade, formed a small retailing operation called The Home and Colonial Trading Association in 1885, with John Musker, a Liverpool shopkeeper as his partner. Julius Drew leaned heavily on Slaughter for legal advice but he was himself one of the most brilliant businessmen of his day. The rapid growth of working class earnings from about 1860 had meant a vastly increased demand for tea, at a time when new sources of supply were being developed in India and Ceylon and import duties remained low. Julius Drew saw that there was an opportunity for the large-scale retailing of tea and a restricted number of other foodstuffs on multiple shop lines at low prices. This course had already been adopted by Sir Thomas Lipton and by The International Tea Company's Stores with great success, but there still appeared to be scope for the creation of a major concern. Drew sought William Slaughter's help in floating a company. Together, in 1888, he and Slaughter transformed The Home and Colonial Trading Association, a business with an issued capital of £2,700, into The Home and Colonial Stores Limited, with one of £197,000. William Slaughter became chairman and remained so until his death nearly 30 years later. Though Home and Colonial began as Slaughter's personal client, it became a client of Slaughter and May as soon as the latter was formed. Its trading operations expanded extremely rapidly: it had 14 shops at the time the company was formed in March 1888, 107 by 1890, 300 by 1900, and twice that by 1914, reflecting, as Julius Drew had so accurately gauged, the strong demand during that period for shops selling

After making a fortune from the creation of Home and Colonial Stores, Julius Drew (1856–1931) retired from business life in the mid-1890s. Two projects occupied his energies thereafter: the magnificent mock-Tudor castle, Castle Drogo, on which Sir Edwin Lutyens worked for 20 years; and the genealogy of his own family. Research on the latter subject led him to alter the spelling of the family name to the Norman form of 'Drewe' by deed poll in 1910.

The Home and Colonial shop front was designed to suggest respectability and reliability. Goods and prices were clearly visible, and the Company's name proudly displayed. (Here it appears on the fascia, across the bottom of the window, on price placards and in the entrance way). There were 600 branches of Home and Colonial Stores by 1914.

a limited range of quality goods at low prices.

The company's accelerated growth was funded by a succession of reconstructions and issues of shares. Its property matters alone were very extensive and brought in fees on a regular basis, but intermittently there were the major financial transactions in which Slaughter in particular was involved. No records survive to indicate how much Slaughter and May earned as Home and Colonial's solicitors until much later, but it is evident that this highly successful enterprise did provide the partnership with a substantial amount of work from the outset.

Possibly because Slaughter and May was in the fortunate position of having a ready-made list of clients right from the beginning, thanks to its connections with John Morris and Home and Colonial Stores, the partners were able to devote some of their attention to the matter of acquiring suitable premises for themselves earlier than would otherwise have been possible. In this they had once again the help of John Morris. Morris's new headquarters in Throgmorton Avenue, an enormous building known as 'The Garden House' because of its proximity to the spacious Drapers' Gardens, was only partially occupied by Ashurst Morris Crisp. The rest was let at rents that covered the cost of Ashurst Morris Crisp's accommodation. With this example before them, William Slaughter and William May decided to follow a similar course. The offices at 18 Austin Friars which the partners occupied in the first two years that they worked together backed onto Throgmorton Avenue, and had probably been chosen in the first instance purely for their proximity to Ashurst Morris Crisp. There was little else to recommend them. Number 18 was merely one of many shabby tenements in a street that housed a jumble of brokers and jobbers, other solicitors, and traders in every commodity from silver to currants. Austin Friars itself took its name from the oldest Augustinian monastery in England, founded in 1253 and destroyed during the Dissolution of the Monasteries under Henry VIII. Though the monastic buildings were long gone by the time Slaughter and May arrived at Number 18, the original church, with its Dutch and Flemish associations, had only been replaced in 1862 following a fire. The street, which bent round the church, was narrow and dimly-lit. In one of London's pea-soup fogs, Austin Friars was an eerie corner of the City.

Slaughter, May and Morris conceived a plan for the redevelopment of Number 18. Only the names of Slaughter and May were to appear on the deeds, as equal owners, but in fact they were each only to own a quarter share of the property with Morris (undisclosed) owning the other half. Between October 1890 and January 1891, the leaseholds of Numbers 16 and 18 Austin Friars and the freehold of Number 17, were purchased. Under the Conveyancing and Law of Property Act of 1881 May and Slaughter were entitled to convert the leaseholds to freeholds which they immediately did. An architect, Frank Hay Roberts (who was the nephew of the former owner of Number 18) was commissioned to design a new building for the

The Dutch Church, Austin Friars, reconstructed in 1862 on the site of its medieval predecessor. It was a City landmark, as well as the most dominant building in Austin Friars, until its destruction in 1940.

site. The old buildings were demolished in the winter of 1890, Slaughter and May having moved into temporary quarters at 21 Great Winchester Street. All of this – the purchases, the demolition, and the design and construction of the new Number 18 – was financed by way of mortgages, of which there were four between 1890 and 1894 for a total of £75,000, to the North British and Mercantile Insurance Company.

The new building was completed by the spring of 1892, and was formally opened on Monday 9th May. It was then, and still is, one of the most attractive buildings in the City, beautifully proportioned and situated along one side of a tiny courtyard off the street. Slaughter and May moved into the second of its four floors. The rest they let. Early tenants included the bankers Seligman Brothers, who had had offices in the old Number 16 and who now took the first floor, the Anglo-Californian Bank, the Munich Reinsurance Company, and a number of other brokers and solicitors. Among the latter was Edward Mihill Slaughter, a cousin of William Slaughter and a close friend of William May.

Net of tax, outgoings and mortgage repayments, the rental of those parts of the new building which Slaughter and May did not require produced about £1,650 in profit for Slaughter and May – nearly £50,000 at today's values. Even so, the partners felt they could do better, and do better they did in June 1896, when they sold the freehold of the property to the United Kingdom Temperance and General Provident Institution (which still owns it at the time of writing) for the sum of £98,000. At a stroke, they cleared the £75,000 mortgage and acquired a substantial amount of capital. At the same time, they set up a private company called Austin Friars Estates, to administer the building, and take a lease of the property from UKPI for 60 years at a fixed rent of £3,502 a year.

The completion of 18 Austin Friars allowed Slaughter and May to display some style in the running of their practice. A chef and a housekeeper for the building were engaged, and the custom of lunching together in the office, probably with the assistant solicitors, began before 1895. Previously May and Slaughter had lunched together out of the office, often at restaurants such as the Café Royal or Simpsons. The partners seem to have agreed that a City firm with an international practice should operate as efficiently as modern inventions permitted. This was a contrast to prevailing attitudes in some – even most – other City law offices, where innovations were resisted. When Slaughter first left Ashurst Morris Crisp he installed a telephone in his own offices. The same number was transferred to the temporary and the new offices, so that Slaughter and May were always accessible by telephone. Typewriters were used from the early 1890s as surviving correspondence on the partnership's notepaper shows. It is interesting to see, on that same notepaper, the firm's telegraphic address, 'Trucidator' ('slaughterer' in Latin) which is still in use today.

Number 18 Austin Friars, designed by Frank Hay Roberts, and built between 1890 and 1892. This building was the home of the partnership until October 1968. The top storey is a twentieth century addition.

23

SLAUGHTER AND MAY.

(TELEPHONE Nº 1025.)
Telegraphic Address:
"TRUCIDATOR-LONDON."

18, Austin Friars, London, E.C.

20th February 1896.

An early Slaughter and May letterhead, showing the firm's telephone number and telegraphic address, 'Trucidator' ('slaughterer' in Latin). Slaughter had previously had this telephone number when he worked from the old Number 18 Austin Friars; the name 'Trucidator' is still used by the firm today.

In his diaries, William May frequently reflected on his personal good fortune. He was right to do so, for there is no doubt that the period from 1890 to 1914 in which his own prosperity and that of the firm was founded was a kind of golden age for solicitors. Their social position was more assured, their professional standing higher, and personal wealth more attainable, particularly in the field of commercial law, than ever before. The reforms of general and legal education effected since 1850 had raised the standard of practice, and with it the status of the practitioner. The increasingly urban character of English life meant that there was more and more call for his services – more property changing hands, more inventions patented and brought to market, more companies formed. And yet by the end of the century the lawyer's working life was more comfortable and productive than his predecessor's of even a generation earlier. Im-

proved communications meant that he could accomplish more in less time. In the week office hours were shorter, since the courts no longer sat in the evenings. It was no longer quite so necessary to live in town. (In 1895 May moved out of London altogether, purchasing a rambling riverside mansion at Send, near Woking, and commuting to the City by pony-trap and train.) It was a period too of remarkable financial stability. The country was on the gold standard, there was virtually no inflation, and taxation, expenses and salaries remained steady. The annual outgoings on 18 Austin Friars, for instance, hardly altered between 1897 and 1907.

For a firm such as Slaughter and May, which specialised in what May called 'financial law', the pressure of work did not fluctuate so much with the law terms and vacations, unless the firm was engaged in litigation. The activity of the market was what determined the pace of life. If market conditions were hectic even the dog days could be frantically busy, as was the case in 1895 when, according to May, he was 'frightfully busy in the office – new work chiefly mining companies are [sic] simply flocking in and for vacation it is wondrous'. In the 1890s and onwards company law provided the greatest opportunity of any field of legal work for the ambitious solicitor. With scores of new companies being formed, there was as much work as they could handle. The fees for corporate work, while difficult to pin down precisely, were certainly much greater than those for either litigation or conveyancing, both of which were time-consuming in relation to the fees they earned.

Ashburton House, Send, near Woking, bought by William May in 1895. The house was a source of great happiness to May. Like his family home at Caversham it had a river frontage, as well as several acres of grounds, with tennis courts, stables and kennels. May's elder son Michael lived there until his death in 1982.

SURREY (*between* **Guildford** *and* **Woking**).—To be Let, or Sold Freehold, a particularly pretty RESIDENCE, of modern erection, well decorated and fitted, and standing in its own charming and nicely timbered old grounds sloping to the river Wey, which affords boating and the right of fishing. The house is approached by a good carriage drive, with lodge at entrance, and contains: *ground floor*, nice hall and staircase, **3 reception rooms**, viz., dining room 24 ft. by 15 ft., drawing room 21 ft. by 15 ft. opening to conservatory, study 17 ft. 6 in. by 15 ft. including bay, also opening to conservatory, fitted lavatory and w.c.; quite shut off are the offices, including kitchen, servants' hall (now used as pantry), larder, dairy, scullery, &c.; *first floor*, seven bed and dressing rooms, bath room (hot and cold supplies), and one attic bed room above. The grounds include tennis lawn for two sets, flower garden, productive kitchen garden, meadow land, green house, &c. The stabling comprises two good stalls and two loose boxes, coach house for two carriages, harness room, and two rooms over for man. Only a few minutes' walk from church and village, with post and telegraph office, and 2½ miles from Woking station, from whence London is reached in about thirty-five minutes.

One of the most useful records of this period for Slaughter and May is an Index to Debited Bills, which names the firm's clients, though not what matter was dealt with. From this Index a number of conclusions can be drawn, the most obvious being the importance, for at least the firm's first 20 years, of the connection with the d'Erlangers. Baron d'Erlanger served as a director, and his firm as bankers, to a number of companies formed during that time to mine gold and diamonds, mainly

This extract from one of Slaughter and May's earliest records, an Index to Debited Bills dating from 1890, shows two of the d'Erlangers' many companies.

in Africa. These companies became clients of Slaughter and May. After 1905, the d'Erlangers were drawn back to South America, and to the Far East. Slaughter and May became solicitors to companies mining gold in Malaya and copper in Chile, and to a steam navigation company operating out of Buenos Aires. George Pauling, originally introduced to the firm by Baron d'Erlanger, himself formed at least four companies which became clients of the partnership in its first 20 years. In much the same way that the relationship of James Morrison and his sons with Ashurst Morris Crisp had proved so

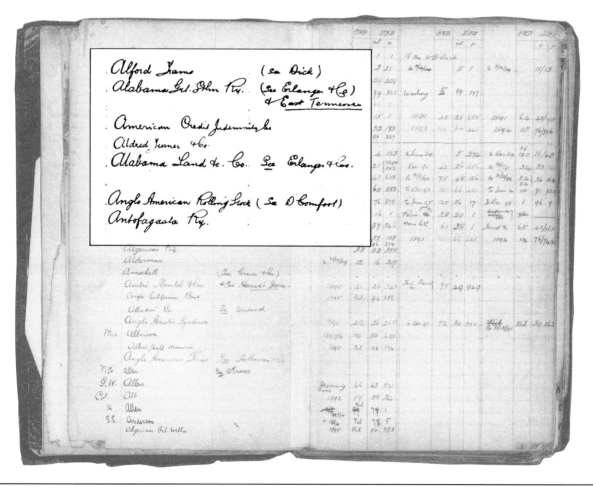

beneficial to the latter firm, so the d'Erlangers' relationship with Slaughter and May was of crucial importance to the early years of the partnership.

The Index also suggests other connections through which the firm acquired its clients. There were a few but important family links, such as Slaughter's with Home and Colonial, but besides the former clients of Ashurst Morris Crisp,

there were groups of client companies active in the same areas, such as brewing, mining and utilities, that gravitated to Slaughter and May. Many of them shared directors, or patronised the same bank. Shared or adjacent premises were another means by which one client sometimes brought another to the firm.

The Index also reveals some interesting facts about the practice. One is the extent to which both May and Slaughter sometimes travelled on behalf of their clients, most often for the d'Erlangers, long before travel became as commonplace, cheap and rapid as it is today. The Index notes

An extract from the Index to Debited Bills showing entries recording the partners' travels on behalf of clients in the 1890s. These particular entries relate to work undertaken for the d'Erlangers, but what matters necessitated these journeys unfortunately does not appear.

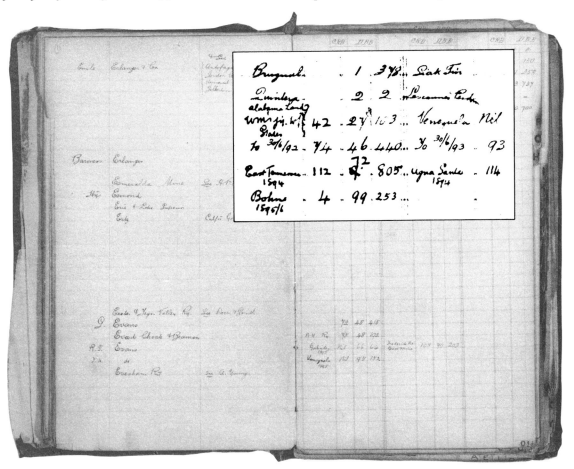

19507

We, Robert Arthur Talbot Gascoyne Cecil, Marquess of Salisbury, Earl of Salisbury, Viscount Cranborne, Baron Cecil, a Peer of the United Kingdom of Great Britain & Ireland, a Member of Her Britannic Majesty's Most Honourable Privy Council, Knight of the Most Noble Order of the Garter, Her Majesty's Principal Secretary of State for Foreign Affairs, &c. &c. &c.

Request and require in the Name of Her Majesty, all those whom it may concern to allow

Mr William Capel Slaughter (British subject)

travelling on the Continent

to pass freely without let or hindrance, and to afford him every assistance and protection of which he may stand in need.

Given at the Foreign Office, London, the 18 day of September 1885

Salisbury

Signature of the Bearer.

W. Capel Slaughter

'WCS's jy to NY', 'WCS's jy to the States', 'WM's jy to Brussels', and 'WM's jy to the States' and in addition Slaughter visited Ireland and Paris. May stood by to go to Chile for the d'Erlangers in 1895, a journey which, had it taken place, would have had him away from Austin Friars for several months. Such private clients as appear in the Index were often persons of some standing. What service Slaughter and May rendered Mr Alfred Nobel, or Mr Joseph Pulitzer, must remain a mystery. T P O'Connor, the Liberal publisher of *The Star*, and Captain O'Shea, whose wife Katharine later became Mrs Charles Stewart Parnell, after one of the most publicised divorce trials of the century, were also clients.

The role of the partners themselves in attracting clients should not be overlooked. Both were personable and spent endless time in the company of business contacts, though Slaughter was probably the more assiduous in cultivating these relationships. Unhappily, he had suffered personal misfortune in 1890, when his wife Ida died, leaving him a widower with three young children at the age of 33. It was not until 1899 that he married again. His wife was Hester Mary Bruce, daughter of the Vice-President of the Port of Calcutta. Three years later, William May married Emma Blount, the daughter of Gilbert Blount, an architect and a member of a leading Roman Catholic family that had owned Mapledurham House, situated on the Thames near Pangbourne, since the

Thomas Galloway Cowan (1866–1943). He became a partner in 1903. A man of monumental stature in every sense, he retired after a brief period as senior partner following the death of William May in 1932.

sixteenth century. At about the same time May and Slaughter enlarged the partnership. The first new partner, George May Simmonds, was a cousin of William May and entered the firm on 1st January 1900 with special responsibility for litigation. He left in 1907 to become a barrister. Thomas Galloway Cowan, admitted in 1887, joined as a partner on 1st January 1903; to him fell the task of dealing with the property matters generated by Home and Colonial at the peak of its growth.

The day-to-day affairs of Home and Colonial continued to demand a great deal of William Slaughter's time, though it seems that at that time May was not involved with the company. Mergers between Home and Colonial, Liptons and

Passport issued to William Slaughter in September 1888. While a passport was not strictly speaking essential at this time, a document such as this could be had on request.

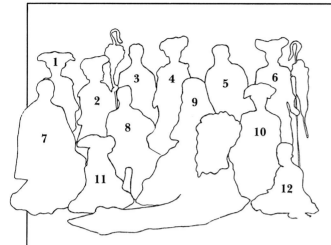

1 Bridesmaid
2 Bridesmaid
3 Edward Slaughter
4 Bridesmaid
5 Sir Percival Radcliffe (Godfather)
6 Bridesmaid
7 Dr Riddle, Bishop of Northampton (Cousin)
8 William May
9 Emma May
10 Margaret Blount (Bride's mother)
11 Dorothy Lacy (Cousin)
12 Ewen May (Nephew)

Adult bridesmaids: Alice May; Marjorie, Louisa and Gilberta Blount

William May's marriage to Emma Blount in September 1902. Edward Mihill Slaughter, centre, was best man.

other firms were mooted on several occasions between 1900 and 1910, in each instance involving Slaughter – and Slaughter and May – in considerable work. Unlike May, who thought nothing of walking 18 miles on a Saturday afternoon as an antidote to a heavy week, Slaughter was prone to bouts of illness brought on by overwork. Even his second marriage did not prompt him to limit his commitments. By 1910 these included,

besides responsibility for many major clients including Home and Colonial, the chairmanships of three investment trusts and a railway company. He was a director of several other investment concerns. His reputation as a lawyer and businessman was by now extremely high, and his breadth of commercial experience widely recognised. All this, of course, reflected well on the partnership. In the years before the First World War, Slaughter's personal standing in the City was one of the firm's greatest assets.

Mayfair and Town Topics, *6th April 1911.*

CHAPTER 3

From the Great War to a Dominant Practice, 1914–1932

In the years leading up to 1914, the threat of war with Germany seemed ever present. By the time it finally came, it had almost ceased to be taken seriously. The nation was psychologically ill-prepared, and the belief that the conflict would be 'over by Christmas' was almost universal. The coming of war and its unexpected continuation seriously disrupted the nation's commercial and banking activities – the very activities that generated legal work for Slaughter and May. Trading on The Stock Exchange was suspended on 31st July 1914, a few days before war was declared. The Exchange remained closed for the next six months, and the corporate and promotional legal work that was Slaughter and May's life-blood drastically decreased. Figures show that bills rendered fell by almost 50 per cent in the first three years of the war, to less than £14,000 in 1917. Like most firms, Slaughter and May probably experienced an increase in matters such as wills, settlements and property sales, the inevitable

result of enlistment and heavy casualties among fighting men.

At a time when three of the leading firms in the City had but four partners each, Slaughter and May had five and was regarded as a large practice. Besides William May, William Slaughter and Tom Cowan, there were two recent additions. The more important of them was William Egerton Mortimer. He is thought to have been brought into the firm by May, but was himself more like Slaughter in his ability to attract new clients.

Mortimer was the son of Canon Christian Mortimer of Lichfield Cathedral. He joined the partnership in 1912 when he was 34, after taking a degree in classics at Christ Church, Oxford, and practising on his own account for eight years. He was to dominate the firm in the 1920s and 1930s and become the City's foremost expert in financial law. The other new partner was Adrian Gray Corbett, who though he was with the firm only a few years, had the distinction of being the first partner to take articles there, with Tom Cowan, from 1908. On the outbreak of war, he joined the Sussex Yeomanry and effectively ceased to practise, though he remained a partner until the end of 1919.

From about this time come the first extensive records of the partnership, and personal reminiscences by former staff. These give an insight into how the firm was run. Saturday working, at least until mid-day, was the rule and would remain so until 1957. Partners took it in turn to come in every other Saturday. On weekdays hours for staff were from 9 a.m. until 6 p.m. though in practice secretaries and clerks carried on until their tasks were completed or until the partners themselves ceased work. One task that seems typical of its time was the conveying of Slaughter's briefcase from the office to his home. Depending on Slaughter's evening engagements, a clerk might be called upon to do this at any hour between 6 p.m. and 9 p.m. If it were after 7 p.m., the clerk received one shilling as 'waiting money'. Regulations were stringent as to time-keeping and dress. Acceptable office wear consisted of a black coat, striped trousers, and white shirt with a starched wing collar.

By 1914 Slaughter and May employed between 20 and 25 persons, all of them male, though perhaps half a dozen employees joined up when war was declared and were away until it ended. The staff included Hugh Pettitt, who would figure prominently as a partner and senior partner in later years. At this point he was an assistant solicitor, having qualified and joined the firm in 1907 after a brilliant mathematical career at Cambridge where he was a senior wrangler. Estate and

Henry Walton joined Slaughter and May in 1909 and stayed until 1955. This picture, taken in 1945, was provided by his son, Mr Anthony Walton QC.

probate matters were his particular interest. Three others whose names stand out are C H Tolley, chief cashier and office manager, and inventor of the famous tax tables; Sidney Disborough, secretary to William Mortimer, a monument of patience and knowledge who was to remain with Slaughter and May for 50 years; and Henry Walton, who handled such litigation as the partnership undertook, and who though unadmitted was known throughout the City as an exceptionally able litigator. Jack Smeaton, much later in his career to head the Litigation department, had at this stage just joined as the office junior, aged 14. Many years later he recorded what a positive impression his first sight of 18 Austin Friars had upon him. As a lad straight from school he knew nothing of the law, but noticed how much grander and cleaner the building was than the other law offices he had seen while looking for work. There was even a uniformed lift attendant. When Smeaton was offered the princely sum of 12s 6d a week – a generous advance on the wage offered anywhere else – the die was cast.

Although business declined so badly during the war, it does not appear that the firm actually laid anyone off, unlike some City practices. A Private Journal which

TELEGRAMS & CABLES. "TRUGIDATOR, STOCK, LONDON."   TELEPHONE Nº⁵ 1775/1776/1777 LONDON WALL.

SLAUGHTER AND MAY

W. CAPEL SLAUGHTER
WILLIAM MAY
T. G. COWAN
W. E. MORTIMER
ADRIAN CORBETT

18 Austin Friars, London, E.C.

2 JUN 1916

M E M O R A N D U M.

Owing to the fact that under the New Military Service Act still more of the staff become liable for military service most of whom have been with the firm for a very long time and to the fact that the smallness of the staff and other circumstances have caused a great reduction in the income of the firm, the Partners feel bound as from Saturday the 17th inst. to reduce the allowances which they are now making, and to substitute the following to married men two-fifths and to single men one-fourth of the salaries which they were receiving before they joined. The allowances will continue for at any rate six months, and the Partners hope to be able to continue them for the duration of the War.

Partnership income declined markedly during the First World War, when business activity was at a low ebb. With the coming of conscription in 1916 the firm was run by a skeleton staff, and was forced to reduce the allowance made to employees in the services.

summarises the partnership's financial affairs between 1914 and 1954 shows that salary levels were maintained throughout the war. In addition to the staff who joined up in 1914, the firm lost others with the introduction of conscription in 1916. The severe reduction in staff brought the first women employees into the firm. The partnership paid an allowance to employees in the Services; what proportion of salaries this comprised is not known until 1916 when the decline in business must have begun to bite, and the respective payments were reduced to two fifths of salary prior to joining up for married men, and one quarter for unmarried. The partners too, apart from William May, were allocated war work. Corbett left the Sussex Yeomanry for the Ministry of Munitions on its formation in May 1915. Cowan assisted Lord Plender in his task as Controller of foreign banks. Mortimer was seconded to the Air Ministry, but not until 1917, fairly late in the war.

Slaughter, on the other hand, was given an important task from the beginning. His appointment to the Royal Commission on Sugar Supplies, officially created on 20th August 1914, was the natural extension of his position as chairman of Home and Colonial Stores. Between this, the affairs of the partnership, and his continuing role as chairman or director of half a dozen companies, there was even less occasion to give himself a rest than normally. Demands on the five-man Sugar Commission were heavy. Its task was to obtain, transport and distribute sugar throughout Britain, a country with the highest per capita consumption of sugar in the world, and whose normal sources of supply from European sugar-beet had been cut off by the war. The Commission was forced to find new ones. All of these – Java, Cuba, Mauritius, the Philippines – were farther away than the usual continental sources, and transport from them consequently more expensive. Keeping prices at a level that working people could afford preoccupied the Commission far more than actually obtaining sugar. With its mandate to 'purchase, sell, and control the delivery of sugar on behalf of the Government, and generally to take such steps as may seem desirable for maintaining the supply', the Sugar Commission was one of the earliest examples of the kind of state control that became so accepted a feature of life during and after the war.

Sugar rationing went on for some time after the war. This card shows weekly entries for 1920 and 1921.

If the coming of war posed protracted problems for the firm, it also posed immediate ones for some of its clients. Under the Aliens Restriction Order of 1914, non-naturalised residents of Britain whose sovereign states were at war with His Majesty were designated 'enemy aliens'. Such persons were only permitted to reside and trade in the United Kingdom subject to certain restrictions, one of which was that they should not carry on the business of banking without the written permission of the Secretary of State. This prohibition directly affected one of Slaughter and May's most valued clients, J Henry Schroder and Company.

Baron Bruno Schroder, head of the firm and one of the City's most respected financiers, was a German citizen at the outbreak of war, although he had long

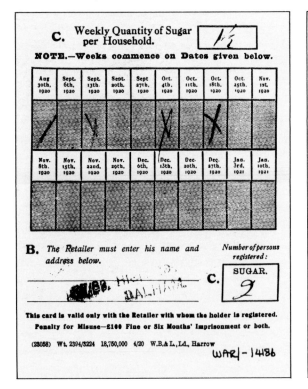

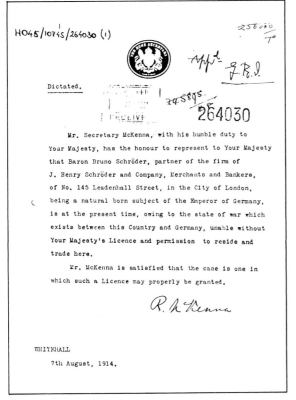

HO45/10745/264030 (1)

Dictated.

264030

Mr. Secretary McKenna, with his humble duty to
Your Majesty, has the honour to represent to Your Majesty
that Baron Bruno Schröder, partner of the firm of
J. Henry Schröder and Company, Merchants and Bankers,
of No. 145 Leadenhall Street, in the City of London,
being a natural born subject of the Emperor of Germany,
is at the present time, owing to the state of war which
exists between this Country and Germany, unable without
Your Majesty's Licence and permission to reside and
trade here.

Mr. McKenna is satisfied that the case is one in
which such a Licence may properly be granted.

R. McKenna

WHITEHALL
7th August, 1914.

Partly as a result of William Slaughter's efforts, a licence was granted to Baron Schroder in August 1914, to reside and trade in England.

been resident in London. The survival of his firm was jeopardised by his German citizenship. As a banking concern, Schroders could no longer carry on its business without a dispensation; and as the property of an 'enemy alien' it could in theory be seized. On 7th August 1914, the day before the banks reopened after a three day emergency closure, Frank Tiarks, Baron Bruno's partner, together with William Slaughter as the Baron's solicitor, and Lord Cunliffe, the Governor of the Bank of England, made an urgent personal representation on Baron Bruno's behalf to the Home Secretary. Slaughter

and Tiarks came armed with counsel's opinion as to the absolute necessity of obtaining a licence for the Baron, whatever assurances they might be given that this was not necessary for a man in so prominent a position. As a result of this forceful approach, Baron Bruno was granted naturalisation and a licence to reside and trade, personally signed by the King, to ensure that there could be no difficulties should naturalisation papers be delayed. The last royal licence to be granted in this way was in 1855, during the Crimean War. Even with his licence, the strength of the anti-German abuse the Baron suffered during the war suggests that his representatives were right to stand firm.

The case of *Ertel Bieber v Rio Tinto*, probably the most important piece of litigation to involve Slaughter and May during the war, also revolved around the question of trading with the enemy. The point at issue was whether certain contracts entered into by the parties before the war had been 'entirely abrogated and avoided' or whether they were merely suspended during the period of the war. The abrogation of the contracts was claimed by Slaughter and May's client Rio Tinto in August 1916 when it brought an action against Ertel Bieber under the Legal Proceedings against Enemies Act of 1915. Rio Tinto won its case. Mr Justice Sankey determined that as of 4th August 1914 the contracts were illegal, since to fulfil them once war was declared would have constituted trading with the enemy. His judgment was later confirmed by the Court of Appeal. The German companies then appealed to the House of Lords on

The date of this photograph is not known, but Slaughter's appearance suggests that it was roughly contemporaneous with the 'CITY LAW' drawing of 1911.

the grounds that suspensory clauses in the contracts deferred their execution only until any so-called 'impediment' – in this case the war – was removed. The House of Lords thought otherwise. The case turned, and the German case was lost, on the point raised by a judgment of 1802, which prohibited a subject from doing any act which might be detrimental to the interests of his own country. It was thought that if an enemy knew that a contract would be fulfilled as soon as a conflict was over, he would be more likely to use the materials in his possession aggressively – in this instance, with adverse consequences for Britain.

Slaughter's work on the Sugar Commission brought him a knighthood 'for services to the nation' in the King's Birthday Honours List of 1915. Tragically, he did not have long to enjoy it. The bouts of ill-health he had suffered since the 1890s were one sign that Slaughter often overreached himself physically. In the autumn of 1916 Slaughter was found to be suffering from cancer. He carried out his business commitments almost to the end, writing a detailed letter to Julius Drew about Home and Colonial matters less than two weeks before his death. He died on 10th March, two months short of his sixtieth birthday. He was buried on 13th March at Kensal Green Cemetery. The same afternoon a memorial service was held at St James's, Piccadilly. Sir George Touche, in a letter to the editor of *The Times*, wrote that 'There was no man in the City whose advice was valued more on any complicated question of law and finance. Ten minutes' consultation with him was worth more than an hour with most men' and on

SIR WILLIAM CAPEL SLAUGHTER.

The Hon. Charles Napier Lawrence and Sir George Touche, M.P., referring to the obituary notice of Sir William Slaughter which appeared in *The Times* of yesterday, write :—

"The death of Sir William Capel Slaughter is an immeasurable loss to the City, where he had long been an outstanding figure. The head of a great legal firm and the chairman and director of important business enterprises, he represented in rare combination legal knowledge and an extensive practical experience of finance and commerce. There was no man in the City whose advice was valued more on any complicated question of law and finance. Ten minutes' consultation with him was worth more than an hour with most men. His brain worked with extraordinary rapidity, and with a fine sense of proportion.

"Carrying the weight of a great legal business, to which problems raised by the war brought many additions, he nevertheless placed his services ungrudgingly at the disposal of the State when war broke out, and they were eagerly availed of. He served on important committees where his quickness and experience and sound judgment were of great value. He worked unremittingly, allowing himself no rest by night or day, and there can be no doubt that his devotion to public duty tended to undermine his strength and handicapped him in the fight against the illness from which he died. . . . For 27 years we were associated with him, in sunshine and shadow. During all that time we never had a semblance of disagreement, but worked together in perfect sympathy and understanding. His friendship has been one of the best things life has given to us. His loss is irreparable and immeasurable, and his death has left a void which will remain always."

W.P. writes :—"For 30 years he was a familiar figure in the City, and his wise counsels, his penetrative business capacity, and the sympathetic and keen interest he always showed in his clients' affairs, carried him to an eminence in his profession which few shared and none envied. It may truly be said that in his long and honourable career as a solicitor he never lost a friend and never made an enemy. But his profession did not absorb all his energies. He was a highly successful man of business as chairman and vice-chairman of important commercial and financial companies, whose prosperity owe much to his well-balanced judgment and sure guidance. There were few qualities which he did not possess, but none shone greater than his capacity for friendship and his enduring, unswerving, and abundant loyalty!"

A tribute to Sir William Slaughter which appeared in The Times *of 13th March 1917.* © The Times, *13th March 1917, reproduced by permission.*

a more personal note, 'His friendship has been one of the best things life has given to us'. One piece of information that appeared several times in the press, not at Slaughter's death, but at May's 15 years later, was that in the whole length of their working life, William Slaughter and William May had never drawn up a formal partnership deed. Though the truth of this will never be known, it seems not implausible, judging from May's diaristic comments about Slaughter, that the partnership evolved out of a relationship that was as much friendship as working arrangement.

Slaughter's absence was the biggest change found by those returning to 18 Austin Friars when the Great War was over. Nearly all those members of the firm who had enlisted did return, though in some cases it was well into 1919 before they were demobilised. Another change from before the war was the presence, for the first time, of women on the staff. All were in clerical or secretarial positions, though men continued to be employed as partners' secretaries. As a small reflection of the loss of so many young men in the war, there were no articled clerks at Number 18 until 1924. Premiums paid for articles had formerly been a healthy source of income for the partnership.

With the lifting of wartime economic controls the City's traditional activities revived, and with them, the fortunes of Slaughter and May. Inflation probably accounted for some of the rise in income and available profits, but records show that in the post-war boom that lasted until the winter of 1920–21, legal work flooded in. The partners also seem to have made some financial decisions, bringing directors' fees into the general pool of income and initiating a generous staff bonus scheme that must have made Slaughter and May one of the City's more attractive

---

BONUS SCHEME

1 In order to mark their appreciation of the services of the Staff and for their encouragement, the Partners have decided to institute a Bonus Scheme, whereby a percentage of the profits of the Firm in excess of a fixed minimum will be set apart for distribution amongst the Clerks as soon as the Accounts have been audited.

2 In order that the Staff may not have to wait for their bonuses until the profits for the year 1920 have been ascertained, which will not be until 1921, it has been decided that the Scheme shall commence as from the 1st January 1919, so that the first distribution will be due in June of this year and will be based on the profits of 1919.

3 Particulars of the Scheme, including the rate of percentage, have been confidentially communicated to the Cashier and will in due course be communicated to the Firm's Auditors.

4 The percentage will be divided amongst Members of the Staff in such proportions as may be decided by the Partners, who reserve the right to exclude any Member or Members from participation if they shall think right.

5 The Senior Members of the Staff will receive their shares of ascertained bonus in one payment and the others either in one payment or in weekly or monthly instalments, if the Partners consider that this course will be more beneficial to them.

6 In view of the exceptional conditions prevailing, the Scheme is a temporary one and applies to the years 1919 and 1920 only. In the course of this year, however, the Partners will decide whether it shall be continued, and, if so, on what basis.

12th January 1920

Memorandum to the staff of Slaughter and May outlining the Bonus Scheme instituted in 1919. Although the scheme was intended as a temporary measure, it remained in force until the 1970s.

employers. The amount of work coming into the firm seems not to have decreased even when the short-lived boom ended. The partnership was enlarged to include Arthur Temple Forman (who because of ill-health remained a partner for only four years) on 1st January 1922, and Hugh Pettitt, who had already been with the firm 16 years, on 1st January 1923. By this time even the junior partner's earnings exceeded by over a hundred pounds the going rate of £1,096 a year for solicitors, and the earnings of the partner next in line were more than double the junior's. It is clear that the partnership continued to prosper during the 1920s.

Though it would be wrong to assume that formal departments existed at this stage, the commercial work that was the parnership's main activity was generally handled by William May and William Mortimer, property matters by Tom Cowan, and estate and probate matters by Hugh Pettitt, though both the latter handled some corporate work. Not surprisingly, May inherited a certain number of Slaughter's appointments. The most important of these was a seat on the Board of Home and Colonial Stores, though he was not to become chairman until 1926. It is reasonable to suppose that some of Slaughter's long-established clients fell to May as senior partner. These included investment companies of which Slaughter had been a director or chairman, but May also took over the Erlanger and Pauling

William Egerton Mortimer (1878–1940) at the wedding of Mr and Mrs W Toler, 2nd June 1936. As senior partner of Slaughter and May from 1933 to 1940, William Mortimer was one of the City's leading solicitors.

interests such as the 'Alabama' companies; Forestal Land, Timber and Railways; and the South American and African mining and railway companies. Investment companies and trusts, together with clients in the electricity supply industry and the motor car manufacturing industry, are known to have been among May's interests.

Despite the number and importance of his clients, May was by the mid-1920s becoming less actively concerned with the day-to-day running of the firm. He had a number of outside commitments, including an involvement in the electricity industry as Chairman of the Greater London and Counties Trust. The real power was gradually passing to William Mortimer, who may rightly be seen as the heir to Slaughter in energy and reputation. Mortimer was an immensely forceful personality. He had great gifts, among them a prodigious capacity for assimilating the facts of a case, and a talent for sizing up the abilities of others. He could glance over a document and identify its essential lines or words – or, with an eye for accuracy that astonished the juniors, the one typographical error.

In the inter-war period Slaughter and May numbered more of the City's great merchant banks among its clients than any other law firm. Together with such long-standing clients as Schroders and Erlangers, the firm acted for Barings, Rothschilds, Morgan Grenfell, and a number of the smaller banks. Many of the banks, but Schroders, Barings and Rothschilds in particular, were involved in making foreign loans and issues to European countries eager to rebuild and modernise their war-damaged cities. Slaughter and May were frequently brought in as solicitors to these issues. The banks were the firm's largest and most active clients and William Mortimer became in turn their most trusted adviser. Like Slaughter, Mortimer came to possess personal influence, in that he knew everyone in City financial circles and was the acknowledged expert in his field. He served on the Council of The Law Society and on many of its sub-committees from 1924. His appointment to the Company Law Amendment Committee, set up by the Board of Trade in 1925 under the chairmanship of Mr Wilfrid Greene, K.C., 'To consider and report . . . what amendments are desirable in the Companies Acts 1908 to 1917' was an important task, as although the Committee recommended very little change in the existing legislation, it conducted the first general and searching review of company law since the Loreburn Committee of 1905.

Mortimer's various commitments meant that he spent a great deal of time moving around the City. With May also much occupied outside the office, there were only Hugh Pettitt and Tom Cowan as regularly resident partners. Pettitt, small of stature, precise in manner and with a memorably dry wit, instilled great trust and loyalty in his clients. He is recalled as working at an old-fashioned reading desk set on a plain table, 'surrounded by tin boxes' containing deeds and indentures. If Pettitt was precise in manner, Cowan was the opposite. He was exceedingly absent-minded, forever leaving his briefcase or umbrella in the train. He was, however, an excellent lawyer with a great following among the clients – Home and Colonial Stores and Rio Tinto were two whose affairs he handled.

The four partners (Forman having left in December 1925) became five, with the addition of Geoffrey Vickers on 1st January 1927, and six when Frank Howard was invited to join a year later. Vickers was something of a celebrity: after Oundle and Oxford, he had won the Victoria Cross at the Hohenzollern Redoubt at the Battle of Loos in 1915 at the age of 21. The strengths of both men were in banking and commercial law. Both were intellectually powerful. Howard was later to become an expert on the law concerning trading with the enemy and exchange controls, and was to write the standard works on both subjects. He was a hefty man, a great oarsman and had an almost photographic memory. Vickers soon came to be known for his ability to compose mentally the text of a lengthy draft which, once dictated, needed scarcely any alteration. South American business seems to have become his speciality fairly quickly. Vickers was tall and spare and exuded energy, both mental and physical. Like May and Mortimer, he was a yachtsman, but in his early days at Slaughter and May a favourite sport was

Sir Geoffrey Vickers V.C. (1894–1982) partner in Slaughter and May 1927–1946. A brilliant solicitor who chose to apply his talents in the wider field of public administration, Vickers was the author of several books, numerous shorter works, and a series of Reith lectures.

Medals awarded to Sir Geoffrey Vickers, now in the possession of the Sherwood Foresters' Museum, Nottingham. The Medal on the far left is the Victoria Cross Sir Geoffrey won at the Battle of Loos in 1915 on his 21st birthday.

William May (1863–1932), co-founder of Slaughter and May.

balltooning, a pastime that got him into occasional scrapes – and into the press.

By the time the partnership was again enlarged on 1st January 1930, this time to nine by the addition of Donald Tewson, Hugh Quennell and Alan Welsford, William May had almost entirely withdrawn from active practice. He was by now in his mid-60s. Staff who joined the firm at the end of the 1920s have only fleeting memories of him. He died on 6th May 1932, two days after his sixty-ninth birthday. He was buried at the private church of St Edward, Sutton Park, near Guildford, on 12th May. The long list of positions he held at his death makes his withdrawal from the firm more understandable. Like Slaughter, May applied his gifts as a lawyer and business adviser widely but he never embraced his profession with the single-mindedness of his partner. He was a man with more interests than the law and finance, as his private life, built around his country estate, his music and his sailing, demonstrated. His other commitments and the existence of Slaughter and May apart, it was also something of an achievement to preserve the way of life he valued, as he had always (on the evidence of his youthful diaries) intended to do.

This tribute to William May appeared in the Berkshire Chronicle, *13th May 1932. Despite having lived at Send, May had not lost touch with the Reading area from which both he and his wife came.*

DEATH OF MR. WILLIAM MAY.

CHAIRMAN OF ELECTRIC SUPPLY COMPANIES.

LEGAL QUALIFICATIONS.

We regret to record the death of Mr. William May, of Ashburton House, Send, Surrey, which occurred on Friday last week at Pitt Hall, Basingstoke. He was the son of the late Dr. George May, a well-known Reading medical practitioner who was largely associated with the Reading Dispensary Association. He was educated at Charterhouse and Oxford University, and, entering the legal profession, he was one of the founders, and at the time of his death was senior partner, of the firm of Slaughter and May, solicitors, of 18, Austin Friars, E.C., one of the largest legal firms in the City of London. He was widely esteemed for his kindly disposition and good fellowship.

The late Mr. May was a director of a number of public companies, being chairman of the Thames Valley Electric Supply Co., Ltd., the Reading Electric Supply Co., Ltd., and Home and Colonial Stores, Ltd. He was also a director of the Greater London and Counties Trust, Ltd., the Wessex Electricity Co., London Express Newspaper, Ltd., Daily Express Building Co., Ltd., and Trust Union, Ltd. He was an outstanding figure and a recognised authority in the legal and financial world, and his knowledge of joint stock company law and practice was of inestimable value to the companies with which he was connected.

His legal qualifications were supported by administrative abilities of a high order, and his keen critical faculties enabled him with remarkable quickness accurately and effectively to appraise the strong and weak points of any scheme or proposition that came before him. It was impossible for him to be other than scrupulously fair in his judgment of men and matters.

Mr. May, who was 69 years of age, was a well-known yachtsman, a keen shot, and a splendid musician. He usually spent the week-ends during the summer aboard his boat, the "Calisaya," on which he greatly enjoyed entertaining his friends to cruises in the Solent and the Channel. He was a member of the Berkshire Club, and until a year or two ago used "The Warren" at Caversham as his summer residence.

The funeral took place at the private church of St. Edward's, Sutton Park, near Guildford, on Thursday. Requiem masses were also said at St. Mary's, Moorfields, Eldon Street, E.C., and at Our Lady and St. Anne's, Caversham.

CHAPTER 4

The 'Mortimer Era' and After

With the increase in the number of partners to ten in 1932 when Howard Millis joined, Slaughter and May was only one partner short of being the largest law practice in the City. The presence of so many Oxford men among the partners was possibly due to the preferences of Mortimer and May for men who had been educated as they had been; Alan Welsford and Howard Millis were both Oxford products and brought the Oxford complement to seven out of ten. Both entered the firm shortly after qualifying as solicitors. Welsford came from a prominent legal family, and was related to several partners in Linklaters & Paines. Quennell too trained in his family's law firm but like Tewson, he practised alone before coming to Slaughter and May. Tewson had in fact practised alone for 22 years before entering the partnership, specialising in tax law. With his arrival the firm gained a rare asset, as tax matters were still generally left to certified accountants and few law firms had their own specialists.

Tom Cowan succeeded William May as senior partner on the latter's death, but for a few months only. Cowan was himself 68 years old, and the real power in the firm lay with William Mortimer. With Cowan's retirement on 31st December 1932, Mortimer became senior partner. While on paper it might appear that this initiated the period of Mortimer's predominance, the 'Mortimer Era', as we have seen, really began in the late 1920s. It was not force of personality alone that would extend it right up to the Second World War. Mortimer excelled at the 'financial law', as William May always called it, on which the firm's original success was based, and he thus continued a tradition built up by the founders. Part of his success lay in recognising and securing for the partnership talents that sustained that tradition. Such men as Geoffrey Vickers, Frank Howard and Alan Welsford, and

Alan Welsford (1900–1987) was admitted as a solicitor in 1926 and joined Slaughter and May as an assistant, becoming a partner in 1930. He was senior partner from 1958 to his retirement in 1963.

later, Christopher Clarke, Hilary Scott, Frank Shipman and Alastair Hamilton, were brilliant lawyers who, though very different from Mortimer and from each other, were his heirs in that they reproduced his exceptional powers of assimilation and judgement.

Of those who became partners during the 1930s, only Christopher Clarke, who entered the firm as an articled clerk in 1928, has written a personal account of the firm between the wars. For much of his time in articles he worked under William Mortimer, or 'Mortie', as he was popularly called, for his kindness was as legendary

as his occasional towering rages and he was regarded with great affection by all but the most intimidated. Working under Mortimer could be exhilarating: foreign loans to exotic-sounding countries and visits to the offices of the City's great financiers added a dash of excitement to the lives of the assistants he selected to work with him. It could also be frustrating – indeed, he was capable of making it deliberately so when he wanted to test the resourcefulness of the junior staff, as Christopher Clarke made clear in the following account of a typical evening at Number 18:

'Mortie was often out for most of the day at meetings and one would be free to get ahead with one's work until the lift gate clanged at some hour in the early evening and his familiar tread could be heard in the passage. Sometimes he would tap on the door with his umbrella *en passant* and that would be the signal to spring to one's feet and follow along to his room to receive instructions . . . A small piece of paper, on which a few words and figures were scribbled by way of an *aide memoire*, would be passed across the table; but, not having been at the earlier discussion with the clients, this gave one little idea of what was required. Mortie, knowing this full well, would nevertheless make a dismissive gesture and say: "There it all is. I'll need the drafts by 10 in the morning for the next meeting" and start to open his evening newspaper. This was merely to tease, and test one's pertinacity, and of course it was fatal to withdraw; one had to stick in one's toes and insist on being given the necessary details or else one was sunk. Quite often, he had more information on some typewritten sheet which he kept in front of him and I, for one, became an adept at reading "upside down"; even if Mortie was going to disgorge the document in his own good time, this trick could be a useful aid to framing pertinent questions.'

Those who developed their abilities to surmount this kind of behaviour found themselves assisting in some of the most demanding and interesting work of the firm. One lengthy matter into which Clarke was drawn through the involvement of Mortimer's clients, the merchant banks, was of international dimensions. Since 1918, the financial affairs of the central European countries had been in disarray. The collapse of the Austrian Credit Anstalt Bank in May 1931, and the declaration by Germany, Austria and

William Mortimer and his wife, the former Cicely Neville-White, at the helm, with unknown crew member, off the west coast of Scotland, probably 1937 or 1938.

Hungary of a moratorium on foreign debts a few months later, caught most of the London banks off their guard. Many had strong German ties and had been lending funds to the German banks and municipalities despite the country's economic instability. When the moratorium was imposed, the London banks were owed enormous sums. (One of the smaller merchant banks, for example, had £4,500,000 in loans frozen in central Europe, as against its capital and published reserves of £1,700,000.)

Many of the banks hardest hit by the German moratorium were clients of Slaughter and May. At their request William Mortimer attended a conference held in Basle in August 1931 to evaluate the financial and economic condition of Germany. At that initial meeting a Foreign Creditors' Committee was formed to represent the foreign banks and a stand-

still was declared with the aim of affording Germany a period of recuperation in which the basis of her economic credit could be restored. The Standstill was intended to last for six months but within that time it became apparent that an agreement for the longer term would be needed. Mortimer's participation in drafting the early agreements reached by the Committee had the result that Slaughter and May regularly accompanied the British banking delegation to subsequent sessions of the Foreign Creditors' Standstill Committee. It was the only firm of solicitors to do so, and there were to be many meetings; the Standstill Agreement of 1932 was the first of a series running right up to 1939. Mortimer, in fact, attended only the 1932 conference, handing over to Geoffrey Vickers and Christopher Clarke after Howard Millis, who had assisted him thus far, moved to Barings.

Matters originating abroad, in countries where the unsettled condition of the world economy was causing difficulties for Slaughter and May's banking clients, did tend to take a long time to resolve. Another that carried on over a period of years was that of the Compañía de Salitre de Chile, commonly known as COSACH. This company was created by the Chilean Government in 1931 to rationalise the Chilean nitrate industry, in which clients of Slaughter and May such as Schroders had been interested since the 19th century. Soon after it was formed COSACH made several issues of bonds, to which a number of the London merchant banks – Barings, Rothschilds, Schroders and Morgan Grenfell – subscribed. The nitrate industry

```
STANDSTILL  SIMPLIFIED
------------------------

A Manual of Self-Tuition

        with

     Vocabulary

Grammar  and Exercises
------------------------




- Price 5 (blocked)  marks -

Payment  may be made (with the
consent of the Reichsbank)  in
any other  currency calculated
at  the official Berlin middle
rate  quoted on  the  second
working day  before the day on
which the purchase is made


    ------------
```

The meetings of the Foreign Creditors' Committee, attended by Geoffrey Vickers and Christopher Clarke, were long and the resolutions that emerged exceedingly complicated. To amuse himself during these sessions, Vickers penned 'Standstill Simplified', with its invaluable guide 'How to speak Standstill . . .'.

was adversely affected by the falling demand for its product that accompanied the world depression, and COSACH was liquidated in January 1933, a scant two years after it came into being. A new company was set up to run the industry and service the bonds COSACH had issued. Attempts to arrive at a scheme of arrangement favourable to COSACH's creditors went on, with a break between 1939 and 1945, for the next 20 years.

In so condensed a narrative, it is not really possible to do justice to the litigation in which Slaughter and May became involved on behalf of clients during the 1930s, but two cases stand out as being of particular interest. The first was the celebrated Royal Mail case of 1931, in which the firm acted for Mr Harold Morland, a partner in the accounting firm of Price Waterhouse, when he was jointly charged with Lord Kylsant, chairman of the Royal Mail shipping group, with having prepared false statements of account. The case concerned the use of undisclosed reserves, the creation of which was a common precaution on the part of many companies seeking to even out fluctuations in earnings from one year to the next. The defence turned on whether a phrase included by Morland in the balance sheet, and which he claimed was there to advise shareholders that reserves had been drawn upon in arriving at the year's results, was – as he asserted – the accepted terminology of professional accountants. In the instance in question, the accounts for the year 1926, reserves had been utilised to transform a trading loss of £300,000 into a trading profit of £439,000.

The trial, held at the Old Bailey from 20th to 30th July 1931 before Mr Justice Wright, with Sir Patrick Hastings as leading counsel for Morland and Sir John Simon for Kylsant, was one of the most publicised trials of the inter-war years. The testimony of Lord Plender, doyen of the accounting profession and a witness for the Crown, was instrumental in showing, first, how widespread was the use of secret reserves by large companies, and secondly, that Morland's phrase was recognised by other accountants in the way he claimed. In the light of that fact, the charge of having wilfully deceived the shareholders could not be sustained, and of that Morland and Kylsant were acquitted. Kylsant, however, received a 12 month sentence on another charge.

Slaughter and May refused a fee for its part in Morland's defence, the partners sharing the widespread feeling in the City that there had been an element of unfairness in the charges laid against Kylsant and Morland. The creation and use of undisclosed reserves was common practice, and although the other directors on the Board of the Royal Mail group had approved the accounts, only Kylsant had been charged. The case had lasting consequences: for the accountancy profession in the contrast it posed between the accountant's purely legal responsibility and a wider moral one, and for company law, which still provided too little guidance for the accountant, despite the re-examination that preceded the Companies Act 1929.

The Royal Mail case was probably the most important in which Slaughter and May had acted up to this time. Another, which cannot match it for its wider significance but which is none the less of interest, was the libel action brought in 1934 by Princess Irina Youssupoff against Slaughter and May's client, Metro-Goldwyn-Mayer Pictures Inc., the makers of a film entitled 'Rasputin and the Empress', which starred no less a personage than Lionel Barrymore. Historically, there had never been any doubt about the identity of Rasputin's murderer; the killing was freely admitted by Prince Felix Youssupoff, the Princess's husband, whose

Metro-Goldwyn-Mayer's Rasputin and the Empress *of 1932 touched off a celebrated libel suit.*

motive was the removal of a patently evil influence over the Russian royal family. The film, however, depicted Rasputin's killer as motivated by revenge for the seduction of his fiancée, a character later shown as his wife. The point in dispute in the case was whether the killer in the film was modelled on Youssupoff; if he was, then the character of the fiancée could reasonably be supposed to represent the Princess. MGM sought to prove that Youssupoff had not killed Rasputin, but when the Prince told his grisly story from the witness box this argument was shattered. The Princess was awarded £25,000

– a sum that showed the jury's awareness of the growing role of the entertainment media in forming public opinion.

The 1930s, especially the middle years, were particularly prosperous for Slaughter and May. Four new partners were taken on between 1935 and 1939; Harry Sporborg and Christopher Clarke on 1st June 1935, Hilary (later Sir Hilary) Scott on 1st July 1937 and Jack Beevor on 1st January 1939, the last man to become a partner before the war. All of them had served as assistant solicitors with the firm since 1930 or 1931. The total number of persons employed by the partnership at this time was about 60, more than twice as many as in 1914.

The war years saw a similar decline in the amount of work coming into the firm

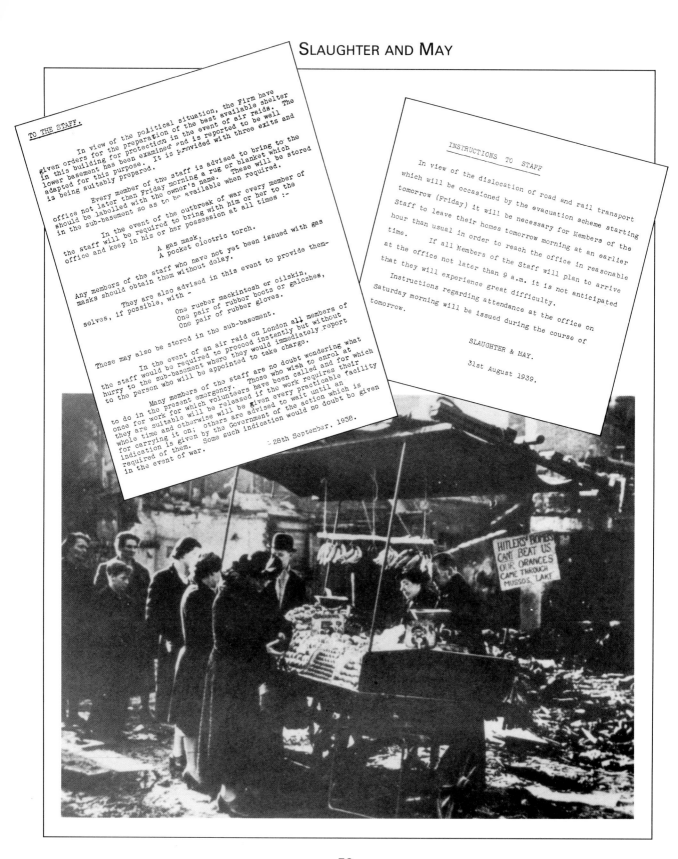

TO THE STAFF.

In view of the political situation, the Firm have given orders for the preparation of the best available shelter in this building for protection in the event of air raids. The lower basement has been examined and is reported to be well adapted for this purpose. It is provided with three exits and is being suitably prepared.

Every member of the staff is advised to bring to the office not later than Friday morning a rug or blanket which should be labelled with the owner's name. These will be stored in the sub-basement so as to be available when required.

In the event of the outbreak of war every member of the staff will be required to bring with him or her to the office and keep in his or her possession at all times :-

A gas mask,
A pocket electric torch.

Any members of the staff who have not yet been issued with gas masks should obtain them without delay.

They are also advised in this event to provide themselves, if possible, with -

One rubber mackintosh or oilskin,
One pair of rubber boots or galoshes,
One pair of rubber gloves.

These may also be stored in the sub-basement.

In the event of an air raid on London all members of the staff would be required to proceed instantly but without hurry to the sub-basement where they would immediately report to the person who will be appointed to take charge.

Many members of the staff are no doubt wondering what to do in the present emergency. Those who wish to enrol at once for work for which volunteers have been called and for which they are suitable will be released if the work requires their whole time and otherwise will be given every practicable facility for carrying it on; others are advised to wait until an indication is given by the Government of the action which is required of them. Some such indication would no doubt be given in the event of war.

28th September, 1938.

INSTRUCTIONS TO STAFF

In view of the dislocation of road and rail transport which will be occasioned by the evacuation scheme starting tomorrow (Friday) it will be necessary for Members of the Staff to leave their homes tomorrow morning at an earlier hour than usual in order to reach the office in reasonable time. If all Members of the Staff will plan to arrive at the office not later than 9 a.m. it is not anticipated that they will experience great difficulty.

Instructions regarding attendance at the office on Saturday morning will be issued during the course of tomorrow.

SLAUGHTER & MAY.

31st August 1939.

Frank Howard (1891–1980) joined Slaughter and May in 1925 as an assistant solicitor and was a partner from 1928 and senior partner from 1952 until his retirement in 1957. A leading expert on banking law and the author of two books, he was known affectionately throughout the firm as 'Uncle George'.

Donald Tewson (1884–1965) was admitted as a solicitor in 1908 and practised alone for many years before joining Slaughter and May as an assistant becoming a partner in 1930. Between the wars and in the late 1950s he was the City's acknowledged expert on the law of taxation and his advice was sought not only by clients but by other law firms.

as had been experienced during the First World War. By the summer of 1940, six of the partners and a third of the staff had entered the services. Mortimer, Pettitt, Tewson, Howard and Welsford were the only partners who remained at Number 18. The bombing of London began with a vengeance in the autumn of 1940. On the night of 15th October it destroyed the Dutch Church that stood as a near neighbour in Austin Friars, and left Number 18 windowless. The building's sub-basement

had been prepared well in advance for use as a shelter, and everyone got used to continuing their drafting or dictation underground when interrupted by the sirens. Documents were ferried nightly to and from Frank Howard's house at Ealing as a safeguard against their destruction by bombing. At Number 18, the partners shared firewatching duties with the staff. Not all the firewatching time was spent on the roof however: the fourth floor of Number 18 was equipped with a billiard

Opposite page – top. **P**recautions against air raids were taken early at 18 Austin Friars. Fortunately the building had a sub-basement, which was equipped as a shelter in the first few months of the war.

Opposite page – bottom. Those who remained in London through the Blitz displayed great resilience to danger and hardship. A sense of humour was never very far under the surface even during the worst conditions.

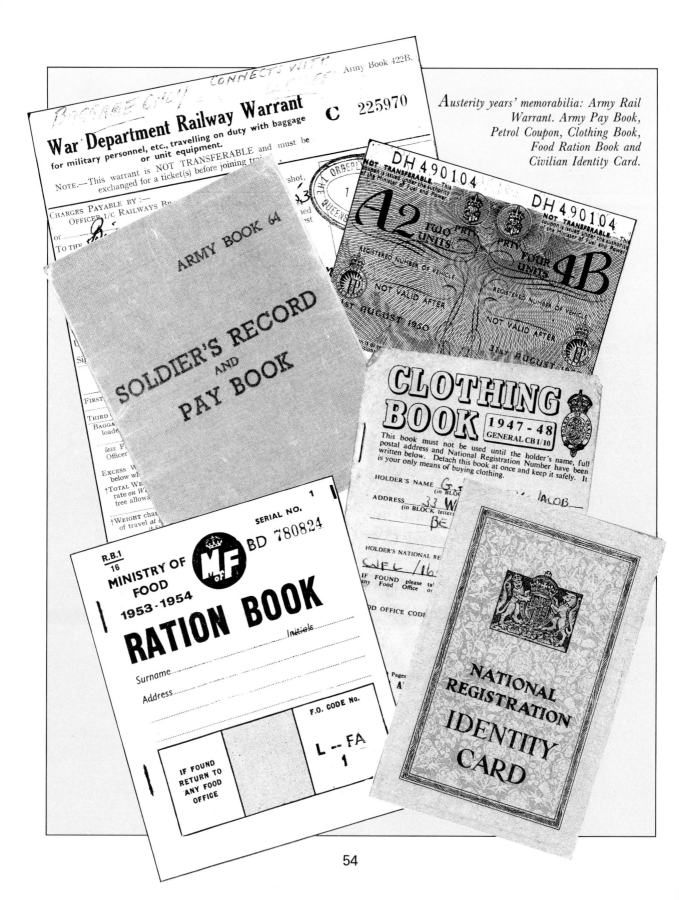

Austerity years' memorabilia: Army Rail Warrant, Army Pay Book, Petrol Coupon, Clothing Book, Food Ration Book and Civilian Identity Card.

Hugh Pettitt (1882–1968) joined Slaughter and May in 1907, became a partner in 1923 and was senior partner from December 1940 until his retirement in 1951. He was the last partner to have known the firm in the days of both Sir William Slaughter and William May.

Frank Shipman (1903–1987) qualified in 1928 and joined Slaughter and May in the same year. He was made a partner in 1941 and remained with the firm until 1965. His exacting standards and high reputation in the City were maintained despite physical disability that was the result of polio in his youth.

table which provided some relaxation for those between shifts.

The death of William Mortimer, on 3rd December 1940, was a severe loss to the partnership. Hugh Pettitt immediately took over as senior partner, and Frank Shipman, an assistant solicitor with the firm since 1928, became a partner on 1st January 1941. With the exception of Christopher Clarke, who had joined the Suffolk Regiment, and those still at Austin Friars, all of the partners had by this time been seconded to the new and highly secret Special Operations Executive, or

SOE. A number of the firm's assistant solicitors also went to 'Baker Street', as SOE came to be called. Its purpose was to co-ordinate non-military, clandestine resistance abroad by means of sabotage and subversion.

Though much has been written since the war about the operations of SOE, of the Slaughter and May men who served in it only Jack Beevor committed his experiences to print, as *SOE Recollections and Reflections*. Under the cover of an Assistant Military Attaché at the British Embassy in Lisbon, Beevor gathered intelligence, kept

Jack Beevor (1905–1987) was a partner in Slaughter and May from 1939 to 1953. Beevor served in SOE and wrote an account of his activities entitled SOE Recollections and Reflections 1940–1945. *He was decorated for his war-time work.*

Harry Sporborg (1905–1985) was a partner in Slaughter and May from 1935 to 1946. Sporborg served as assistant to General (later Sir Colin) Gubbins in SOE and was decorated by four governments for his war-time services.

track of secret activities in Spain, and laid plans for the destruction of key resources in the event of a German invasion of Portugal. The life he led was very different from that at Austin Friars, but, as he comments with a touch of irony in his book, his training as a solicitor served him well. Harry Sporborg held a position which, if less dangerous than Beevor's, was as close to the centre of SOE's administration as it was possible to get. As deputy to General (later Sir Colin) Gubbins, chief of SOE from September 1943, Sporborg was intimately concerned with both the facilities and the operations

sides of the organisation. Another person who served with distinction with SOE in the field but who joined the firm after the war and subsequently became a partner was Bob (later Sir Robert) Clark. His Commanding Officer was Hilary Scott and his wireless contact, Marjorie Lewis, subsequently became his wife. Of the other partners, Geoffrey Vickers also held positions of outstanding importance, ending the war as Director General of the Economic Intelligence Division of the Foreign Office.

One matter of note to come the way of the partnership during the war was

Sir Hilary Scott (born 1906) joined Slaughter and May on his admission in 1930, became a partner in 1937 and remained with the firm until 1974. He was first elected a member of the Council of The Law Society in 1948 and, having served on many of its committees, became President in 1966.

Christopher Clarke (born 1907) joined Slaughter and May as an articled clerk in 1928, became a partner in 1935, and was senior partner from 1964 until his retirement in 1971. His memoirs – and memories – of the firm, from the 1930s onwards, are an invaluable source of information.

the arbitration over the sum paid to Courtaulds Limited as compensation for the enforced sale of its American subsidiary, the American Viscose Company. The sale was requested in March 1941 by a British Government desperate for funds to pay for munitions and anxious to placate the isolationist lobby in the United States, which refused American aid until Britain had brought all of her own resources into play. Courtaulds bowed to the Government's request solely to secure the passage through the United States Senate of the all-important Lend-Lease Bill.

The original award to Courtaulds – £16,700,000 – was a good deal less than the value the company placed on its subsidiary. The arbitration took place in July 1942 before Mr Justice Simonds. The company asked for £30,000,000 – and was awarded £27,125,000, a great improvement on the earlier award.

All of the partners, with the exception of William Mortimer, survived the war. Inevitably, the firm lost some of its members on active service, though fortunately, very few. Christopher Clarke had probably the most unpleasant war

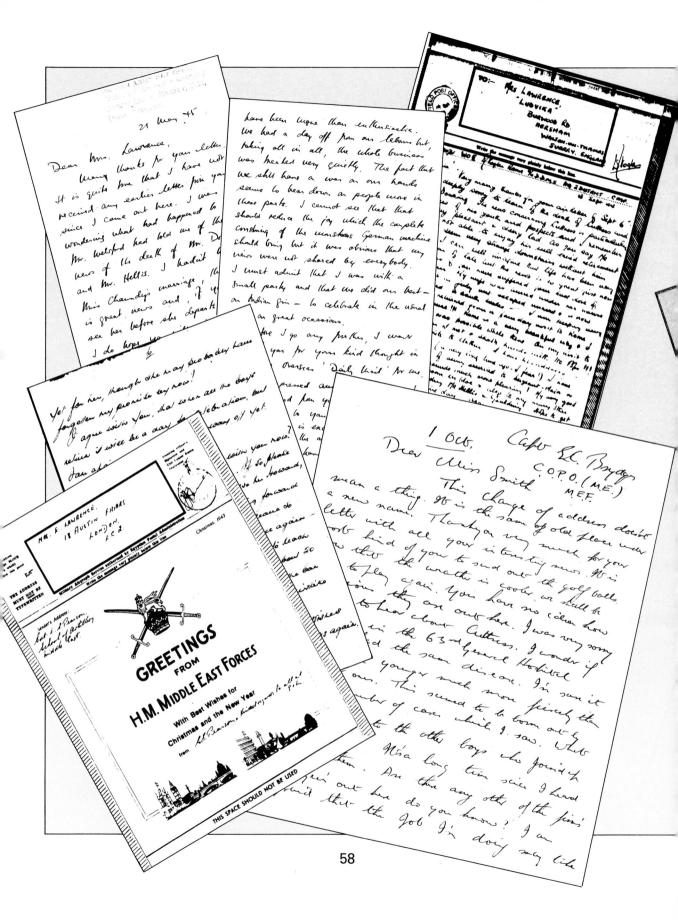

21 May 45

Dear Mrs. Lawrence,

Many thanks for your letter. It is quite true that I have not received any earlier letter from you since I came out here. I was wondering what had happened to ... Mr. Welsford had told me of the news of the death of Mr. D... and Mr. Hellis. I hadn't ... Miss Chaundy's marriage, the ... is great news and, if ... see her before she departs ...

I do hope ...

have been more than enthusiastic. We had a day off from our labours but, taking all in all, the whole business was treated very quietly. The fact that we still have a war on our hands seems to bear down on people more in these parts. I cannot see that that should reduce the joy which the complete crushing of the menacing German machine should bring but it was obvious that my views were not shared by everybody. I must admit that I was with a small party and that we did our best — an Indian fin — to celebrate in the usual ... on great occasions.

... I go any further, I want ... you for your kind thought in ... Overseas 'Daily Mail' for me.

Yet for her, though she may probably have forgotten my promise by now! I agree with you, that when all the boys return it will be a day ... celebration, but ... I am afraid ... away off yet.

TO: Mrs. Lawrence.
"LUDVIKA"
BURWOOD RD.
HERSHAM
WALTON-ON-THAMES
SURREY. ENGLAND

MR. E. LAWRENCE.
18 AUSTIN FRIARS
LONDON.
E.C.2.

Christmas, 1943

GREETINGS
FROM
H.M. MIDDLE EAST FORCES

With Best Wishes for Christmas and the New Year
from ...

THIS SPACE SHOULD NOT BE USED

1 Oct.   Capt ...
Dear   C.P.O. (M.E.)
Miss Smith   M.E.F.

This change of address doesn't mean a thing. It is the same old place under a new name. Thank you very much for your letter with all your interesting news. It is just the kind of you to send out the golf balls. Now that the weather is cooler we shall be able to play again. You have no idea how ... they are out here. I was very sorry to hear about Cuthross. I wonder if ... in the 63rd General Hospital ... the same disease. I'm sure it ... younger such more fiercely than ours. This seemed to be born out by ... number of cases which I saw. When ... to the other boys who joined ... them. Are there any other of the fins' ... out here do you know? I am ... that the job I'm doing very like ...

Elsie Smith, known to all as 'Smithie', was Slaughter and May's telephonist from 1918 until 1948. During the Second World War, she kept up the tradition set by Charles Tolley in the First, by writing letters and sending Postal Orders and parcels from the firm's 'Fund' to staff in the Forces. Some of the war-time correspondence, of which the above is only a small sample, still survives. Smithie married Arthur Lawrence, who became head of the Costs department.

The Dutch Church, Austin Friars, was destroyed by bombing on the night of 15th October 1940. This is the scene which met the eyes of anyone looking out on the Friars.

of anyone in Slaughter and May as a Japanese prisoner of war for three and a half years. He, like many others, was amazed on his return to London at the extent of the devastation. The ground-plan and character of the City would never be the same. There were plenty of 'registered offices' that consisted of no more than a doorstep; the old shortcuts from one client's office to another were largely obliterated. The ruins of the Dutch Church dominated Austin Friars. Number 18 at least was still standing – even if, with boards over many of the windows, it looked less elegant than usual.

There were plenty of 'registered offices' that consisted of no more than a doorstep but '. . . Winding Up Petitions had according to the Winding Up Rules to be served at the Registered Office of the Company . . .'.

CHAPTER 5

The Post-War Challenge,
1945–1967

It was not until the war in Europe had been over for nearly a year that Slaughter and May was back to full strength. Demobilisation took until well into 1946, and while at first it seemed that the temporary staff taken on during the war would be released when the men they were replacing came home, by the time that happened business was picking up, and the replacements found themselves permanent members of staff.

The first few years after the war were as austere as any that had been endured during it. Everything was in short supply, particularly coal and paper. Such coal as could be obtained was mostly dust, so that there were no fires. For much of the time, there was no light. The high-ceilinged rooms at Number 18 were hard to heat at the best of times; in the winters of 1946 and 1947 – the latter an especially cold one and beset by a fuel crisis – people worked in their coats in shadowy rooms, some of

which still had boards over the windows. Every scrap of paper and every envelope was re-used. Rationing was still in force and even bread now came on the ration. A former articled clerk has described a shop near Austin Friars 'where for a few shillings you could have your clothes turned inside out and rebuffed to make them look a little less threadbare. We lads obviously couldn't afford that sort of thing, but the Partners did and I at all events was very impressed.' The partners' luncheon room managed to provide reasonable fare as it was classified as a catering establishment and as such was exempt from the food rationing regulations. For the articled clerks however, lunchtimes were a problem, 'largely through the absence of anything worthwhile to eat and the absence too of anything with which to purchase it'. Acceptable places to eat in the bombed City right after the war were few and far between: the articled clerks went to one cheap restaurant until they noticed that a three inch ledge at about picture rail level was a race track for the local rats.

This kind of frugality was probably harder on the younger members of the firm, many of whom had been in the services and came back from the war imbued with the longing for a new, fairer and more prosperous society. For the time being, all that had to wait. For the articled clerks in particular it was a struggle to survive financially once the £300 premium for articles and stamp duty of £80 were paid. One articled clerk recalls handing over his money at the Stamp Office around the corner from Austin Friars, where the official commented that 'he hoped the young man's training was worth it, and that he got his money back some day'!

One effect of the war that gradually came to be felt was a marked lessening of the formality that had attended relations between partners and staff in Mortimer's day. Those who had been in London through the war had whiled away the same long hours firewatching together and had seen a different side of one another, whether partner or office boy. This is not to say that differences of status evaporated, but only that, as among the population at large, people of very different backgrounds and levels of responsibility came to know one another better than before.

One example of this was the encouragement given to some members of the staff to improve their standing in the firm. Even before the war there had emerged several who had shown such outstanding ability that they were offered articles. While the firm had no policy of giving leave so that

*F*red Edmonds (1903–1985) joined Slaughter and May as a boy in 1919 and was offered articles in 1929. He was admitted in 1946 and became a partner in 1949. Edmonds was the first partner to work his way up to a partnership from a junior position, and the first partner to be with the firm for more than 50 years.

members of the staff could study for their examinations, several of the partners did provide as much training as they could within the confines of the work to be done. Some men did, by dint of much hard work in their own time, become admitted solicitors, and two became partners. They were Fred Edmonds, who joined Slaughter and May as an office boy and served his articles under Hugh Pettitt, was admitted in 1946 and made a partner in 1949; and Edmund Belton, who was similarly trained by Donald Tewson. Belton became

Edmund Belton (born 1911) joined Slaughter and May as a boy in 1927, completed his articles after the war and was admitted in 1948 and made a partner in 1952. He succeeded Donald Tewson as one of the City's leading experts in taxation law and, like Fred Edmonds, was with the firm for 50 years.

a partner in 1952 after 25 years with the firm and only left after another 25 years. His reputation in the tax field, like Tewson's, carried considerable weight in the City.

Some of the men who returned after six years of military life found the transition to their former positions uncongenial, and left the firm. The departures were not restricted to the staff. Three of the partners, Geoffrey Vickers, Harry Sporborg and Hugh Quennell, also left. Quennell set up a financial and legal consultancy in Tokenhouse Yard, a few steps away from Number 18. Sporborg, who for his work with SOE was appointed CMG

and received American, French and Norwegian decorations, moved to Hambros Bank as a director in April 1946. Vickers received a knighthood in the 1946 New Year's Honours List for his wartime service to economic intelligence. He had returned to Slaughter and May when the war was over, but a growing interest in public administration led him to accept the position of solicitor and legal adviser to the National Coal Board, then in the process of being formed, in July 1946. Three new partners were elected on 1st July 1946, bringing the numbers back up to 12. Alastair Hamilton, educated at Marlborough and Oxford and articled to Hugh Quennell from 1932, had been an assistant solicitor with the firm since 1936 and was one of those who had spent the war in SOE. Stephen Constance completed five year articles in 1935 after being educated at Tonbridge, and joined Slaughter and May on his admission. Edward Brydges completed his articles with the London firm of Smith and Hudson in 1932 after obtaining both a BA and BCL from Oxford, and practised alone for three years before entering the firm in 1935.

The changes that took place within the firm after the war reflected the new and increasing demands of commercial legal practice. One change was the growth of departments to handle specific areas of law, such as conveyancing, tax, probate and trust work and, later on, pensions. The Conveyancing department set up by Edward Brydges in 1946 was the first of the deliberately created, functional sections headed by partners that came into being after the war. Up until then, most

Alastair Hamilton (1908–1985) joined Slaughter and May in 1932 as an articled clerk and was admitted in 1936. During the war he served with SOE. He became a partner in Slaughter and May in 1946, retiring in 1969. During that time he was one of the firm's leading commercial partners.

Edward Brydges (born 1907) joined Slaughter and May in 1935 and was a partner from 1946 until his retirement in 1974. He took charge of the Conveyancing department on its formation in March 1946 and was the Senior Conveyancing Partner for nearly 30 years.

of the partners handled any concerns regarding property that arose in connection with their banking or corporate clients, just as they each concerned themselves with wills, settlements, probate and trusts when necessary. But the rebuilding and development of land after the war, especially in London, brought much new property business to Slaughter and May. These matters were in addition to the property-related affairs of longer-standing clients. Lost or destroyed records, boundary disputes and discovery of ownership where there had been loss of life were factors that made some of the work very time-consuming. It quickly became evi-

dent that if all conveyancing previously handled by partners on behalf of clients was passed to a new department, the work could be dealt with more efficiently. The total of such work was large and was to grow larger with each passing year. By the mid-1950s the department was severely undermanned for the amount and complexity of the work it did. John Gurney became the second conveyancing partner in 1955.

The growth in property work was paralleled in other areas, mainly because of the increasing number of clients attracted by the firm. William Mortimer, so it is said, believed that a society dominated by bureaucracy would emerge from the war, a society in which government regulation would swamp enterprise, and the kind of legal work for which Slaughter and May was known would all but disappear. The first part of his prophecy came true with the great changes in the relations between the state and industry that followed the war. Because the reconstruction of industry was hampered by balance of payment problems, regulation was kept on in an effort to arrive at a more favourable balance of payments. The nationalisation of important sectors of the economy also proceeded apace under the Labour government.

Mortimer was wrong, however, to forecast the decline of the City law practice. Company mergers in some industries, under the pressures of international competition and increased demand in the home market as the austerities of the immediate post-war years gave way to the more stable 1950s, increased the amount of work for solicitors. Slaughter and May already numbered many of the largest companies in the country as clients together with groups of companies in the same industries, such as brewing, film distribution, and motor car manufacture. Even in the austere economic climate of the late 1940s many smaller companies sought funds for expansion, and came to Slaughter and May for advice when they decided to go public. The firm's already notable number of American clients expanded considerably after the war and through the 1950s. Some of these connections arose through the American banks such as Morgan Guaranty and Bank of America, which were also clients of Slaughter and May. The number of American banking clients was to grow substantially during the 1950s and 1960s as more of these banks opened branch offices in London. Within the partnership many of these were dealt with by Frank Howard, whose expert knowledge of the law relating to exchange controls was highly valued; and later, by Peter Marriage. Personal contact and word of mouth were as important in attracting clients as they had ever been; just as the American banks gravitated to Slaughter and May, so too did the banks of many developing countries as they established themselves in London. The firm's largest and most active clients, after the war as before it, were the London merchant banks. To these important links with the City's financial aristocracy, Slaughter and May has owed much of its resilience to the economic ups and downs of the post-war period. To the ranks of banking clients for whom it had acted for many years before the Second World War, it has added new ones, notably S G Warburg & Co.

The increase in the number of clients inevitably brought an increase in the number of partners and staff. Three more partners, Fred Edmonds, Bob Cooper and Peter Marriage were appointed on 1st January 1949. Malcolm Bell and Colin McFadyean became partners on 1st January 1951, bringing the number to 15. Hugh Pettitt, whose career stretched all the way back to 1907, retired as senior partner on 31st December 1951 and was succeeded by Frank Howard. Just as with conveyancing up to 1946, each partner had up to this time acted when necessary on probate matters for his own clients.

None the less this was an area in which Pettitt had taken a strong interest, and new clients bringing this kind of work to the firm were usually dealt with by him. After his departure, probate and settlement work also came to be handled by a small department under the general supervision of Edward Brydges. With the addition of Edmund Belton in 1952 the partnership gained a strong second to Donald Tewson, and the broadening of his tax specialisation into another small but distinct department. Tewson's retirement in 1956 left Belton in charge of the Tax department, which handled personal and corporate tax, estate duty, and some wills and settlements.

It was not only the heightened pressure of work that made the creation of departments both sensible and inevitable. The law in many areas was becoming so complex that specialisation among the partners was seen as one means of reducing the risk of error. Increasingly the profession was subject to what one partner has called a 'flood of law-reforming legislation', and it was no longer possible for each partner to be fully acquainted with all of it. Even the creation of additional partners to handle the volume of work – ten new partners were appointed between 1955 and 1961 – did not alleviate this problem.

These appointments, together with several retirements, brought the total number of partners to 20, the legal limit of partnership size, thereby creating another difficulty for the firm. After the war the senior men had been concerned to recruit younger partners to avoid the situation of one City practice known to them, in which the succession had all but died out. With the limit on size reached, there was a real danger that excellent lawyers would be lost to the firm through lack of prospects for advancement. In the early 1960s this did occur, with many young men who had completed their training at Slaughter and May departing for smaller firms or for jobs in companies or City institutions. While a number of partners left during the same period to join the merchant banks which were themselves beginning to compete with solicitors in arranging public issues, this still did not leave enough vacant partnerships for the number of young solicitors to whom the firm would have liked to offer them.

During this period the number of staff also rose steeply, from a head count of about 120 in 1946 to about 220 by 1960. The increase had the inevitable result of crowding 18 Austin Friars to the point where additional space outside it had to be found. To some extent the growth of departments made this easier both to effect and to accept, though perhaps for the departments chosen to move it was less acceptable than for others! Conveyancing was the first to go, initially into rooms immediately opposite Number 18, then to quarters in Throgmorton Avenue. There were several additional moves and in no case were the arrangements entirely satisfactory until space became available in 24 Austin Friars. Litigation, which on the retirement of Henry Walton was brought entirely under the direction of Jack Smeaton, also moved in the late 1950s, to 6 Austin Friars, next to the recently restored Dutch Church.

Changing conditions demanded not only greater specialisation and more

Jack Smeaton joined Slaughter and May during the First World War, in September 1915. He remained with the firm until 1967. This picture of him in later years was taken at the wedding of Peter Morley-Jacob in July 1962.

space, but greater efficiency in record keeping and clerical methods within the practice. The old 'press-copy' system gave way to the hand-cranked duplicator after the war, making possible for the first time multiple copies of documents typed on special waxed stencils. The problem of preserving exact copies of letters was solved when one of the partners devised a novel form of partnership letter-paper, whereby one headed sheet and two carbon copies were held together by a perforated strip along the top. In the early 1960s, the partnership took the unusual step of commissioning a business efficiency firm to carry out a survey of office procedures. As a result of the survey, antiquated practices such as the daily recording of incoming and outgoing letters in enormous ledgers,

at a great waste of time and energy, were finally done away with.

At about the same time several innovations in legal practice came into being. One was the introduction of 'Verification Notes' for prospectuses. These took the form of a series of questions based on the draft prospectus, designed to ensure that not only were factual statements contained within it properly checked, but also that inferences which could be justifiably drawn from them were correct too. This procedure was invented by Jack Beevor and was widely adopted by other City practices and is still in use today. Because of the size of the partnership and its client list by the early 1960s, the possibility that two partners might inadvertently find themselves instructed by clients engaged on opposite sides of the same matter was very real. This became a potentially dangerous situation during the spate of takeovers and mergers that took place about this time. A register in which each partner was expected to record matters on hand and to search for conflicts of interest before taking on new clients was one attempt to prevent this. Another new development was the Information Room, which established a client register and a system of information storage and retrieval designed to help the user to identify precedents for transactions and documents. The number of clients on which data was held by 1966 was over 2,500.

By the mid-1960s, the firm was desperate for space. Unfortunately the attempt to acquire the lease of 14 Austin Friars coincided with the rebuilding of The Stock Exchange dealing floor in Throgmorton Street, and The Stock Exchange took over

18 Austin Friars, the home of Slaughter and May from 1889 until 1968.

Number 14 instead. Slaughter and May then took several floors in a building belonging to Morgan Grenfell at 72 London Wall. The conclusion was inescapable; by now the solution to the firm's accommodation problem was to leave Austin Friars. This decision, however difficult, was to prove easier to make than to implement.

CHAPTER 6

'The *City Firm . . .*' – *the past twenty years*

The year 1967 marked a watershed for Slaughter and May, as it did for so many professional partnerships. One hundred and five years after the Companies Act of 1862 imposed a limit of 20 partners on the size of solicitors' partnerships, the Act of 1967 removed this restriction leaving law firms free to respond to a changing business scene by determining their own optimum size. Slaughter and May breached the former barrier at the first opportunity, with the appointment of four new partners on 1st January 1968. Since then the firm has taken in an average of three or four partners a year.

Though no one knew it at the time, 1967 was also Slaughter and May's last full year at 18 Austin Friars. The prospect of a further growth in numbers brought the accommodation problem to a head. A solution to the overcrowding at Number 18 and the inconvenience of having departments lodged under various roofs nearby finally materialised when the Registrar's department of the National Provincial Bank vacated 35 Basinghall Street. Slaughter and May took over the whole of these premises, which were more than twice the size of Number 18, and moved there in October 1968. The new building was a scant five minutes' walk away from Austin Friars, standing to the west of Moorgate and Coleman Street, close to Guildhall. In character, the premises and the area in which they stood were far removed from the charming corner of the pre-war City that was Austin Friars. The area west of Moorgate and either side of London Wall had been bombed almost flat during the war. The new buildings that had risen on the ruins of the old were mainly of the stark and functional kind so typical of the post-war period. Most people in Slaughter and May accepted the firm's departure from Number 18, its home for the whole of its existence, as a necessity, but a regrettable one. There was no doubt however that the

35 Basinghall Street, which Slaughter and May has occupied since 1968.

new accommodation was appreciably lighter and brighter than the old and the benefits of having the whole firm under one roof were immediately felt.

It can hardly be an exaggeration to say that the period from 1967 to the present day has brought more changes to the conduct of business in the City than have occurred in any previous period. These changes have affected the whole business community and, while they have occurred too recently to be seen in any real historical perspective, they have clearly had enormous implications for City law firms.

The increase in the amount of legal work being generated and its greater complexity, due to a steadily enlarging body of legislation, has made heavy demands on City practices. The most obvious result is that firms have become much bigger.

Slaughter and May itself, at the close of its first century, has 77 partners. More than half of them act in the firm's traditional area of commercial law, but another consequence of rapid change is that the others work in areas that have generally increased in importance during the past 20 years – and indeed, in some which did not exist 20 years ago.

These changes inevitably had an effect on how the firm was run. Traditionally, the senior partner administered the firm

St Giles Cripplegate—

*T*op picture, extensive bomb damage in the City, looking west towards the eventual sites of 35 Basinghall Street and Austral House. The Barbican now stands on the area between Moorgate Station and St. Giles Cripplegate.

*B*ottom picture, the area rebuilt.

35 Basinghall Street

St Giles Cripplegate

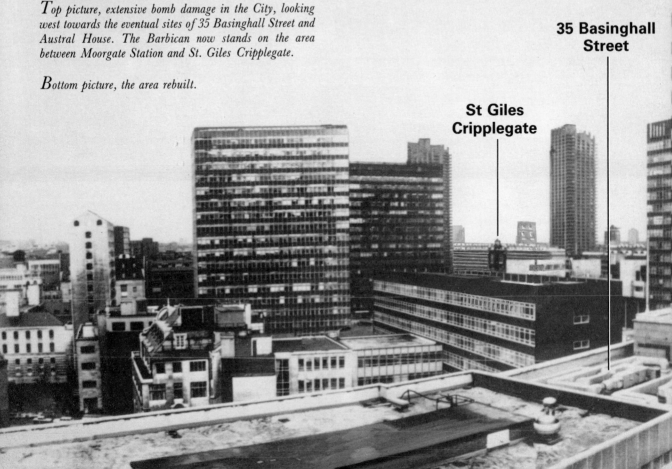

on a day to day basis, assisted by the Chief Accountant on financial matters and the Office Manager on property and personnel matters. More important matters were discussed by a Management Committee, which consisted of the five most senior partners present in the office on the day an *ad hoc* meeting was called, and crucial decisions were taken by the whole partnership. By the late 1960s, the administration of the firm had become exceedingly time-consuming. Senior partners found it virtually impossible both to deal with their clients and to be freely available for consultation with colleagues in the way that was accepted practice in the firm. The burden of administration had come to include such matters as the allocation of new clients, finding and filling office space, the engagement of assistants, interviewing prospective articled clerks, and a host of other demands. The first improvement on this system was the appointment in 1969 under Christopher Clarke of an administration partner, whose task was to relieve the senior partner of much of the everyday burden. In the early 1970s the composition of the Management Committee was changed to include representatives of the less senior levels of the partnership. The resulting structure, apart from minor alterations, remained unchanged until 1986.

The developments of the last 20 years have been so numerous, rapid and complex that it is not possible to give more than an outline here of the effects they have had on the firm. Another consequence of the increase in legislation and the size and business of the partnership has been the further growth of departments whose subject areas complement the firm's major activity, corporate and financial law. Since the mid-1960s large annual amounts of new legislation in, for instance, the area of taxation have meant that legal practitioners have had constantly to update their knowledge of this ever more detailed subject. As a result the Tax department has had both to expand in terms of numbers and to relinquish certain ancillary matters with which it formerly dealt. This in turn helped to bring about the creation in 1965 of a Trust department, to which work devolved from both the Tax department and the Conveyancing department, and shortly thereafter a Pensions department. The Pensions department went on to develop an expertise in the related areas of employment law and profit sharing and share incentive schemes.

From the later 1960s there also evolved, within the far larger commercial area, a specialisation in competition law both domestically and in the wider context of the European Economic Community. This followed the earlier establishment of an office in Brussels, a step undertaken by the firm in the belief that the Treaty of Rome would soon affect many of the areas in which Slaughter and May advised its clients. The rejection of Britain's application to join the Community was a set-back to this conviction and the decision was taken to close the Brussels office early in 1965 and to handle affairs relating to the EEC from London. Because of improved communications this proved such a satisfactory solution that the decision was not reversed even after Britain's entry into the Common Market in 1972. In recent years the EEC group has formed a separate department and, in conjunction with the Litigation department, has developed a further specialisation in the law relating to intellectual property.

Even in departments that had existed for some time, such as conveyancing, the nature of work was gradually altering. Up until the 1960s much of the department's work was concerned with conveyancing spin-offs from commercial matters and with freehold and leasehold property work on behalf of existing commercial clients, some of whom were among the nation's largest property developers and financial institutions. From being mainly a service department for the benefit of the commercial side of the firm, in the 1970s it became a front-line department in its own right, with the scale of matters handled increasing immeasurably, and attracting new clients for the firm. Planning, development and construction expertise were added to the areas previously covered. Some of the property development matters in which the department has been involved in recent years have been on the very largest scale and include the Broadgate development near Liverpool Street Station and the new Canary Wharf development in Docklands.

Broadgate, where Slaughter and May acted for British Railways Board. This is one of the largest single comprehensive developments in the City since the Great Fire of London.

Slaughter and May has never been a firm in which departments were hard and fast, or in which specialisations were narrowly interpreted. The practice's strength, historically and currently, has been in commercial law and the areas that have emerged in the past 20 years have both served, and latterly fed, the firm's work in this predominant field. Unlike many large firms, Slaughter and May has made a conscious choice – manifested in the very composition of the partnership – to avoid over-specialisation. In all areas the aim has been to preserve something of the traditional 'generalist' approach, where legal practitioners handle all aspects of a matter from start to finish. The modern structure of the Commercial department – five working groups, each comprising several partners, assistants and supporting staff – lends itself to providing, when required, teams drawn from across the department so that on large matters flexibility is achieved without seriously depleting any one working group.

Not surprisingly, it has been the Commercial department that has felt the weight of change most acutely, and has had to adapt most to keep abreast of it. The economic policies of successive governments, inflation, the broader economic climate worldwide, and advances in communications have all been factors in altering the business environment. Change has manifested itself in a host of different ways. In times of economic expansion many companies have grown larger through mergers and acquisitions. The increase in activity in this field in the mid-1960s led to the establishment in 1968, under the auspices of the Bank of England,

of the Panel on Take-overs and Mergers and the publication of the original version of the City Code. Over the years the City Code has been expanded and refined so that it now represents a sizeable field of practice in its own right.

Methods of capital raising by companies, an area which has always been of special interest to Slaughter and May, have undergone marked changes. A once-popular method was the issue of debenture stocks, until runaway inflation put an end to the willingness of institutions to subscribe large sums at fixed rates of interest. In the 1970s the debenture stock market all but dried up, apart from stocks offered by way of consideration for takeover bids, though in recent years, with inflation once again under control and more stable interest rates, there has been a modest revival of activity. In the international market, the business of syndicating loans had developed principally because by the 1960s many international loans had become so large that no single financial institution could make them alone. In the 1960s and 1970s syndicated loans accounted for a major part of Slaughter and May's banking work but in recent years they have given way to more sophisticated financial instruments with names such as RUFs (Revolving Underwriting Facilities), NIFs (Note Issuance Facilities) and MOFs (Multi-Option Facilities).

Not only have methods of financing changed, but the sources of funds have changed too. A major development during the last 20 years has been the expansion of the Euro-currency market (funds, predominantly US dollars, deposited outside their home countries). With the increase in

Examples of offer documents for takeovers with which the firm has been concerned.

international trade and the removal of exchange controls, companies which relatively recently would have restricted their borrowings to the domestic market now make full use of the Euro-currency market both for short term loans, such as Euro-Commercial paper, and longer term loans, such as notes and bonds.

On both the domestic and international fronts, the firm has participated in project financing. Slaughter and May was in-volved early on in the opening up of the North Sea for exploration and particularly in the financing of the Forties Field, the first UK financing arranged on a 'produc-tion payment' basis. Overseas, notable projects have included the Bougainville Copper Mine project in Papua New Guinea and the Woodside North-West Shelf project and the Ranger Uranium Mine project, both in Australia.

As the examples suggest, the scale of matters undertaken by commercial lawyers today are of a size undreamed of two decades ago. This growth in scale has

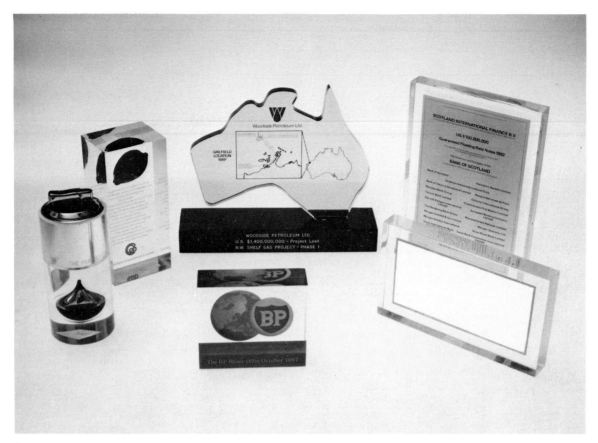

It has become the custom for the principal participants in major financings to receive a memento, usually in the form of an acrylic block, of the transaction. The block normally contains a copy of the prospectus or of the 'tombstone' but more imaginative mementos, such as those containing samples of the end product (e.g. oil from the Forties Field or uranium ore from the Ranger Mine) have been devised.

been matched by the speed at which work can, and must, be carried out. In the days when Slaughter and May still occupied 18 Austin Friars, most correspondence was produced on manual typewriters, duplicated by means of carbons or hand-cranked machinery, and delivered by post or by hand. Clients requiring draft documents accepted that preparing them might take a week. The arrival of the photocopier and the word-processing system as standard equipment has changed all that. The production of successive drafts within hours, to be transmitted almost instantaneously around the world by the use of facsimile, is now taken for granted.

If the speed at which matters can be dealt with has had a profound effect on the lives of solicitors, so has the more frequent need to travel on clients' affairs, due to the degree to which their businesses have become international. Slaughter and May has always had strong connections abroad due to the international interests of its clients and, as we have seen, from the early days of the partnership, partners did on

An aerial view of the Ranger Uranium Mine at Jabiru in the Northern Territory of Australia. Slaughter and May represented the banks who provided the major part of the debt finance for this project, generally regarded as one of the most advanced of its type in the world.

occasion travel on behalf of clients. These journeys were, until the 1960s, generally regarded as major undertakings, in terms of time as well as financially and physically. Recent advances in air travel have changed all this. For the past 15 years, it has been a rare week when there have not been half a dozen representatives of the firm on the move. The pressure on time today probably means that a lawyer who has just flown in from Tokyo – having made this journey there and back in a matter of days – is likely to come to the office straight from the airport.

This increased activity abroad has been paralleled by the establishment of Slaughter and May's own branch offices overseas. The Brussels office, as has been mentioned, was short-lived. Operations in Paris, on the other hand, have proceeded successfully from January 1973, when the firm's first representative arrived there, through the arrival of the first resident partner and the official opening of Slaughter and May's office in January 1974, to the present day, when there are five partners and some 25 staff in impressive quarters on the Boulevard Haussmann.

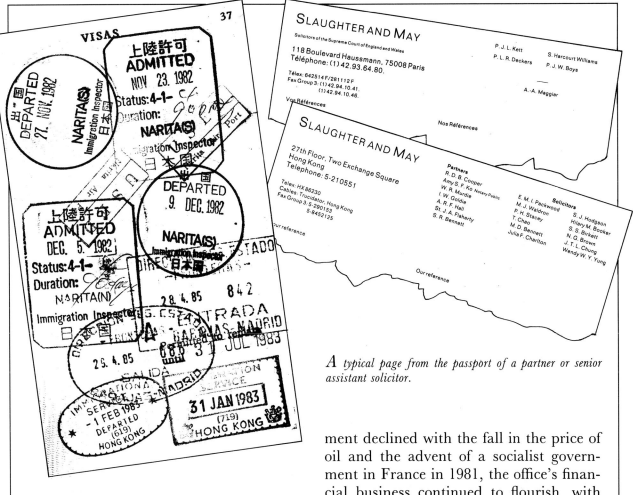

A typical page from the passport of a partner or senior assistant solicitor.

118 Boulevard Haussmann, Paris 8ᵉ. Slaughter and May occupy the building from the first floor upwards.

Initially the work in Paris consisted mainly of advising British companies which were investing in France but, following the rise in the price of oil in the mid-1970s, it rapidly expanded as a result of the considerable reinvestment of western funds by the oil-producing countries. The Paris office was well placed to assist clients concerned with the investment of 'petro-dollars' in the French speaking world. While this kind of invest-

ment declined with the fall in the price of oil and the advent of a socialist government in France in 1981, the office's financial business continued to flourish, with clients from Latin America and Africa replacing those from the Middle East. The partners based in Paris are among the firm's most travelled – one of them recalls a week in which he caught 16 flights, interspersed with meetings. Passports issued to these partners frequently run out before their time simply because of the number of visas acquired.

At about the same time as the Paris office was set up, the decision was taken to open an office in Hong Kong. Slaughter and May was the first City firm to establish itself in the Colony. In August

Below, Two Exchange Square where the firm's offices are situated.

Above, the Mass Transit Railway Corporation, constructor and operator of Hong Kong's underground railway system, was one of the Hong Kong office's first clients. The firm has acted for the Corporation in many of its financing arrangements and a number of its construction contracts.

Colin McFadyean (born 1914) joined Slaughter and May in 1937 as an articled clerk, became a partner in 1951 and retired in 1982. After a long period as Vice-Chairman and Chairman, he is now a Councillor Emeritus of the Business Law Section of the International Bar Association.

Peter Marriage (born 1915) joined Slaughter and May in 1936 as an articled clerk. He was admitted in 1946, made a partner in 1949 and was senior partner from 1972 to 1975. Like Frank Howard, his principal expertise lay in the field of commercial banking.

1974, one partner and two assistant solicitors, together with supporting staff, began working from offices in the Connaught Centre. As a new independent force in the Hong Kong legal community, Slaughter and May had to establish a practice from scratch. Independence, however, meant that there was no conflict of interest when prestigious clients such as the Hongkong Bank required its services. Another important early client was the Mass Transit Railway Corporation, builders of the Hong Kong underground system, for which Slaughter and May acted in negotiating financing arrange-

Opposite, one of Cathay Pacific's fleet of Rolls Royce-powered Boeing 747s at Kai Tak International Airport. Slaughter and May were solicitors to the offer when shares of Cathay Pacific were offered for sale to the public in 1986.

ments and a number of construction contracts. While the nature of the work of the Hong Kong office has always had a strong bias towards banking and corporate finance, there have been occasions when, as evidenced by the work done for the Mass Transit Railway Corporation, conveyancing has been a significant area, as has litigation. Today the Hong Kong office has six partners and a total staff of approximately 80. The firm has become so well established in the Hong Kong business community in the past 14 years that one of its partners recently served as President of the Hong Kong Law Society.

Prime movers in setting up these early ventures abroad were Colin McFadyean, whose wide acquaintance was most helpful to the firm in this regard, and Peter Marriage, who succeeded Christopher

Keith Wright (born 1920) joined Slaughter and May as an articled clerk and was admitted in 1950, becoming a partner in 1955. He was senior partner from 1976–1984.

Clarke as senior partner on 1st January 1972 and retired at the end of 1975. Peter Marriage's term and that of his successor, Keith Wright, covered a period when geographical expansion was recognised as being necessary to maintain Slaughter and May's ability to serve an increasingly international body of clients. It also coincided with the technological revolution, and both information services and the means of carrying out day to day work were radically updated to take advantage of the latest systems.

With the recent volume of new legislation and the tendency for primary legislation to be in broad terms, leaving the detail to be covered by statutory instruments, practice notes and guidelines, prompt access to the latest publications has become essential to the firm's practice. The library and the information room provide indispensable back-up to the firm's practitioners.

The newest additions to the firm's branches abroad, the New York office and the Tokyo office, have both been established within the past five years. The decision to operate from New York was taken because Slaughter and May's connections with the commercial and investment banks in that city had increased so dramatically that to have an office there seemed a natural extension of the partnership's identity. The office opened on 5th November 1984, occupying half a floor of a mid-town office block, Tower 56, at 126 East 56th Street. Tokyo too had become such an important financial centre by the mid-1980s that a presence there was considered to be essential. The partnership's office in Tokyo was also intended to serve as an additional location in the Far East to Hong Kong. Opening a branch in Japan was a step the partners had considered for

some time but the restrictions on the activities of foreign lawyers that prevailed until April 1987 had made this impracticable. Even under the new legislation, foreign lawyers are restricted to practising within a specified area of foreign law in which they are recognised by the Japanese Ministry of Justice as qualified to practise, and they are not allowed to employ or take into partnership Japanese lawyers. Despite these constraints, and the high

costs of operating in Tokyo, the partnership is confident of the future for its second Far Eastern office, which opened on 1st March 1988.

In addition to opening offices overseas, the firm has acquired further accommodation in London. In 1972 the firm overflowed from 35 Basinghall Street into certain floors of the adjoining 4 Coleman Street and further floors were leased between 1973 and 1978. In 1981 and 1982 parts of a neighbouring building, Gillett House, were occupied by the Property department and certain groups within the Commercial department. In 1986 the opportunity arose to acquire by stages the whole of Austral House, on the other side

Austral House, where the Commercial and Tax departments of Slaughter and May are located. The continued expansion of the firm in the past 20 years has meant that 35 Basinghall Street has long been outgrown.

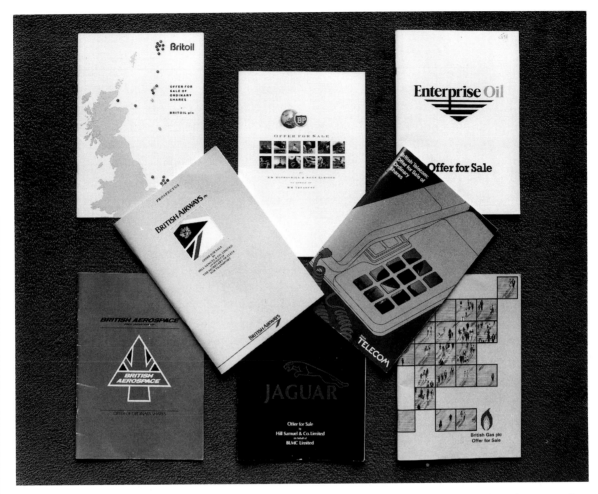

A major area of activity for Slaughter and May in recent years has been that of privatisations. There have been few since 1981 in which the firm has not been involved.

of Basinghall Avenue from Number 35, and this now houses all the Commercial groups and the Tax department. Most recently, the firm has taken a lease of the newly constructed building at 16 Coleman Street and connected it to 35 Basinghall Street at two levels. The Litigation department moved into this building in April 1988.

One of the most significant new areas in which Slaughter and May has been active in recent years has been that of privatisations. From 1981 onwards the firm has acted, either for the company being denationalised or for the bank advising HM Government, in a succession of privatisations, including British Aerospace, Amersham International, Associated British Ports, British Airways, Enterprise Oil, Sealink, Jaguar and British Telecom. The last-named was the first of the really gigantic privatisations, and brought with it challenges of a corresponding magnitude. It occupied more people for a longer and more intensely laborious period than any previous matter, and demanded the co-ordination of efforts and timing on an international scale. All of this stood Slaughter and May in excellent stead when the firm was instructed by HM Government in connection with the sale of further shares in British Aerospace, Britoil and BP and the privatisation of British Gas. The firm has been instructed by the company on the British Steel sale and most recently by the Department of Energy in relation to the privatisation of the electricity industry. However demanding, these transactions have proved extremely stimulating to the partners and staff who have worked on them. The association with these matters has not only reflected positively on the partnership's capabilities, but has also allowed it to build up a level of experience in the field of privatisations that is second to none.

The changes and growth in Slaughter and May's sphere of activity in recent years might suggest that members of the firm have been able to spare little time for the affairs of the legal profession as a whole, or those of the wider City community. Nothing could be less true. A number of partners have served as active members of committees of The Law Society, most notably Sir Hilary Scott who, as a member of the Council from 1948 until his retirement in 1971, served on numerous committees and as President of The Law Society in 1966–67. He was also a member of the Jenkins Committee, which was appointed by the Board of Trade to review company law. It sat from 1959 to 1962 and recommended, among other things, the lifting of the limit on partnerships' size which was enacted in 1967. Tony Mallinson, who succeeded Keith Wright as senior partner in June 1984, was a member of the Banks Committee, appointed in 1967 by the Board of Trade to examine the British patent system, Chairman of the Cinematograph Films Council from 1973–1976 and Legal Adviser to the Accounting Standards Committee from 1982–1986. Nicholas Wilson served as a member of the Committee of Inquiry on Industrial Democracy (the Bullock Committee) of 1976.

A number of partners have held positions within the International Bar Association. Sir Hilary Scott was the first Vice-Chairman of the Business Law Section from 1970 to 1971. Colin McFadyean served as Vice-Chairman from 1971 to 1974 and as Chairman from 1974 to 1976. He is now one of its Councillors Emeriti. Tony Mallinson has been a member of the Council of the Section since 1984. Besides serving as officers of the committees of the Association, partners regularly contribute papers at its conferences.

Partners have also been associated with the work of the Solicitors Benevolent Association since Sir William Slaughter's day. At any one time several partners are usually members of the various committees of the City of London Solicitors Company in the areas in which the firm takes a particular interest, such as banking, company law, land law, intellectual property and revenue law. Members of the firm have also been elected to the Court of Common Council of the City of London, and the partnership has a close connection with the nearby church of St Lawrence Jewry. The various solicitors' dining clubs

Left, the Slaughter and May band not only provides 'in-house' entertainment but also performs at outside functions. It has become a regular feature of the City of London Solicitors Company's float in the Lord Mayor's Show.

Above and left, the canteen which is also a popular venue for presentations, Christmas parties and other social occasions. The fact that it is open from 7 am to 9 pm is an indication of the length of the current working day in the City.

Tony Mallinson (born 1923) joined Slaughter and May as an articled clerk, was admitted in 1952 and became a partner in 1957. He was senior partner from 1984 to 1986. Although senior partner for only two years, he was responsible for a major overhaul of the firm's constitution.

George Inglis, the current senior partner, joined Slaughter and May as an articled clerk, was admitted in 1960 and became a partner in 1966. He succeeded Tony Mallinson as senior partner in 1986.

also number partners among their members and there is a long tradition for individual partners to serve on the boards of charitable and scholarly organisations.

Although Tony Mallinson was senior partner for only two years, having adhered to the retirement date he had chosen many years earlier, he set in motion a full-scale restructuring of the management of the firm to achieve an administration more responsive to changing needs. Today the firm is run by a Partnership Board consisting of the senior partner, George Inglis, who took over from Tony Mallinson on 1st May 1986, three executive partners representing the areas of finance, systems and personnel, and four non-executive partners drawn from different levels of the partnership.

Within the firm, time has been made for the creation of a positive working atmosphere. Articled clerks are regarded as the life-blood of the firm and are chosen with a view to their eventual succession as partners. The firm deliberately selects articled clerks who, in addition to high academic qualifications, have strong interests outside their chosen profession. Clubs for drama and numerous sports, a jazz band and a choir, as well as chess, bridge and countless ad hoc clubs, draw participants from all levels of the firm and are an important means by which staff become acquainted. A canteen is another useful way of bringing staff together. Relations between senior and junior staff are more informal today than in past years, with first names normally being used throughout the firm. Among professional staff, the 'open door' policy means that all members of the partnership, however senior, are accessible to assistant solicitors and articled clerks for advice and discussion. These are features of the firm's working life which everyone is determined to conserve, however demanding the future may prove.

That the high standing of the firm is recognised by others is shown by the description of the firm given in a recent publication, *The Legal 500*, 'To many people, Slaughter and May is "the" City firm. It has a very high reputation in the City and in the business world, and, perhaps more significantly, in the legal world.'

As the partnership achieves its first centenary, the intention of its partners is as it has been since the days of William Slaughter and William May – to maintain the firm's standing at the top of the legal profession, and to do so with singular style.

Partners

1.1.1889	W. C. Slaughter	10.3.1917	1.1.1949	P. Marriage	31.12.1975
1.1.1889	W. May	6.5.1932	1.1.1951	A. M. Bell	30.6.1976
1.1.1900	G. M. Simmonds	31.12.1907	1.1.1951	C. McFadyean	31.12.1982
1.1.1903	T. G. Cowan	31.12.1932	1.1.1952	E. Belton	31.12.1975
1.1.1912	W. E. Mortimer	3.12.1940	1.1.1955	R. A. Clark	30.9.1961
1.1.1914	A. G. Corbett	31.12.1919	1.1.1955	W. J. S. Gurney	31.12.1966
1.1.1922	A. T. Forman	31.12.1925	1.1.1955	E. Lyall	12.5.1960
1.1.1923	H. Pettitt	31.12.1951	1.1.1955	T. P. Walmsley	3.1.1980
1.1.1927	C. G. Vickers	15.7.1946	1.1.1955	K. E. Wright	30.6.1984
1.1.1928	F. C. Howard	31.12.1957	1.1.1957	A. W. Mallinson	30.4.1986
1.1.1930	D. C. Tewson	31.12.1956	1.1.1957	R. G. Norton	30.4.1986
1.1.1930	H. Quennell	3.6.1941	1.1.1958	J. D. Simon	30.6.1984
1.1.1930	A. M. Welsford	31.12.1963	1.10.1961	G. Ll. Law	31.12.1967
1.1.1932	C. H. G. Millis	25.2.1933	1.10.1961	G. G. Williams	30.6.1966
1.6.1935	H. N. Sporborg	6.4.1946	1.1.1964	J. W. Tapner	
1.6.1935	R. C. G. Clarke	31.12.1971	1.1.1966	S. R. Ward	
1.7.1937	C. H. Scott	31.12.1974	1.1.1966	T. G. M. Buckley	
1.1.1939	J. G. Beevor	31.12.1953	1.9.1966	G. B. Inglis	
1.1.1941	G. F. Shipman	31.12.1965	1.4.1967	B. E. Russell	30.6.1983
1.6.1946	J. A. S. Hamilton	31.12.1969	1.1.1968	A. F. Flower	31.12.1979
1.6.1946	E. C. Brydges	31.12.1974	1.1.1968	R. G. A. Youard	
1.6.1946	S. J. Constance	30.6.1953	1.1.1968	H. C. Rumbelow	
1.1.1949	F. W. Edmonds	31.12.1969	1.1.1968	N. S. Wilson	
1.1.1949	C. F. Cooper	30.9.1964	1.1.1969	A. M. H. Smart	

1.1.1969	R. C. Harvey		1.7.1980	T. A. Kinnersley	
1.1.1969	P. J. Morley-Jacob		1.7.1980	R. A. M. Welsford	
1.1.1969	G. Turner	30.4.1987	1.7.1981	D. J. Beales	
1.1.1970	G. F. Renwick		1.7.1981	J. E. F. Rushworth	
1.1.1970	L. St. J. T. Jackson		1.7.1982	M. G. C. Nicholson	
1.1.1970	F. J. Wilson		1.7.1982	S. M. Edge	
1.1.1971	M. Read		1.7.1982	N. P. G. Boardman	
1.1.1972	F. W. Neate		1.7.1983	J. Hine	
1.1.1972	T. J. B. Pallister		1.7.1983	T. N. Clark	
1.1.1973	G. P. Balfour		1.7.1983	I. W. Goldie	
1.1.1973	N. N. Jacobs		1.7.1983	M. Hughes	
1.1.1973	R. R. Montague-Johnstone		1.7.1983	G. W. James	
1.1.1974	C. J. V. Robson		1.7.1984	E. A. Codrington	
1.1.1974	M. S. E. Carpenter		1.7.1984	R. M. G. Goulding	
1.1.1974	R. R. S. Beaumont		1.7.1984	A. R. F. Hall	
1.1.1975	P. J. Langley		1.7.1984	C. J. Hickson	
1.1.1975	R. D. B. Cooper		1.7.1984	A. J. R. Newhouse	
1.1.1975	G. I. Henderson		1.7.1984	G. E. S. Seligman	
1.1.1975	M. J. D. Roberts		1.5.1985	J. H. Savory	
1.1.1975	T. G. Freshwater		1.5.1986	P. F. J. Bennett	
1.1.1976	H. M. Nowlan		1.5.1986	St. J. A. Flaherty	
1.1.1976	G. D. Child		1.5.1986	R. M. Fox	
1.1.1976	C. F. FitzGerald		1.5.1986	D. T. Frank	
1.1.1977	G. P. J. Finn		1.5.1986	H. R. Jacobs	
1.1.1977	J. S. Haw		1.5.1986	F. M. Mitchell	
1.1.1977	M. Pescod		1.5.1986	C. J. Saunders	
1.1.1978	J. B. D. Rowe		1.5.1986	C. F. I. Saul	
1.1.1978	P. J. Robson		1.5.1986	R. J. Thornhill	
1.1.1978	C. Hall		1.5.1987	G. J. Airs	
1.1.1978	G. M. Ridley		1.5.1987	R. N. S. Grandison	
1.7.1979	P. A. S. Grindrod		1.5.1987	C. R. Smith	
1.7.1979	P. T. Jennings		1.5.1987	G. P. White	
1.7.1979	J. H. Macaskill		1.5.1988	N. J. Archer	
1.7.1979	R. Slater		1.5.1988	A. G. Balfour	
1.7.1980	P. J. L. Kett		1.5.1988	C. M. Horton	

Acknowledgements for illustrations

Page 1, signatures of William Slaughter and William May, by courtesy of National Westminster Bank PLC.

Page 4, entry in the *Kent Directory*, 1796, for Bruckshaw & Capel; page 4, entry in *Lowndes London Directory*, 1788, for William & Edmund Slaughter, Cheesemongers; page 6, entry in *Post Office Directory*, 1842, for Capel & Slaughter, coal merchants; page 7, 'Railway Speculators'; page 8, title page of *Railway Intelligence*, 1857; page 21, the Dutch Church – all these by courtesy of Guildhall Library, City of London.

Page 6, Mihill Slaughter, by courtesy of The Stock Exchange and Guildhall Library, City of London.

Page 9, John Morris; page 16, Morris/Slaughter agreement – both by courtesy of Ashurst Morris Crisp.

Page 14, William May as a young man at Oxford; page 15, William May's music; page 25, Ashburton House; pages 30–31, William May's wedding – all by courtesy of Robert May, Pitt Hall Farm, Basingstoke.

Page 18, Baron Emile d'Erlanger the elder; page 18, Baron d'Erlanger the younger, William Slaughter *et al.* at dinner – both by courtesy of Rodolphe d'Erlanger.

Page 19, Julius Drew, by courtesy of Anthony Drewe.

Page 20, Home and Colonial Stores – shop front, from J B Jefferys, *Retail Trading in Britain, 1850–1950* (1954) by courtesy of Cambridge University Press.

Page 22, from a painting of 18 Austin Friars by Edward Bawden RA.

Page 36, sugar ration cards, by courtesy of J Sainsbury PLC, with thanks to Bridget Williams.

Page 37, licence granted to Baron Bruno Schroder, PRO reference HO 45/10745/264030. Crown Copyright material in the Public Record Office is reproduced by permission of the Controller of HMSO.

Page 41, William Mortimer at the wedding of Mr & Mrs William Toler, by courtesy of Mr & Mrs Toler.

Page 43, Sir Geoffrey Vickers, provided by his grandson, Paul.

Page 43, medals of Sir Geoffrey Vickers, photograph by courtesy of Sherwood Foresters' Museum, Nottingham.

Page 45, obituary of William May, reproduced from the *Berkshire Chronicle*.

Page 48, William Mortimer and his wife, by courtesy of Christopher Clarke.

Page 51, still photograph from *Rasputin and the Empress*, by courtesy of Turner Entertainment Co.

Page 52, 'Hitler's Bombs Can't Beat Us', from Joanna Mack and Steve Humphries, *The Making of Modern London 1939–1945, London at War* (Sidgwick & Jackson, London, 1985), by courtesy of the Imperial War Museum.

Page 54, Austerity years' memorabilia, with thanks to Peter Morley-Jacob.

Pages 58–59, picture and war-time correspondence, by courtesy of Elsie Lawrence.

Page 61, '. . . Winding Up Petitions', drawn by Ed Keeble.

Pages 72–73, bomb damage in the City and the area rebuilt, © Times Newspapers Ltd.

Page 79, the Ranger Mine, by courtesy of Energy Resources of Australia Ltd.

Various other photographs taken by Graham Silvester.

Index

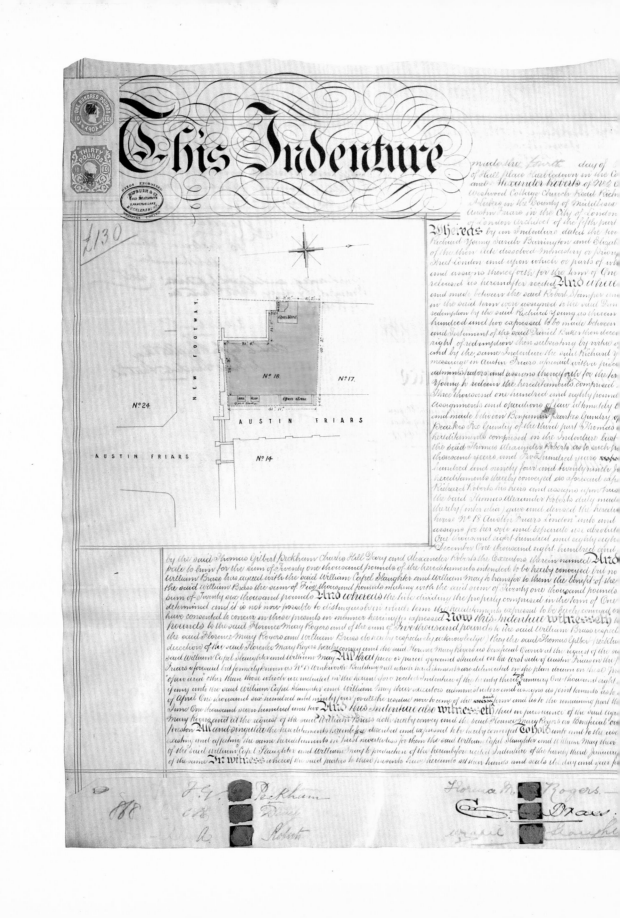

This Indenture

made the fourth day of ... of Hall Place Hartledown in the Co... and Alexander hereits of N° 4 ... Westwood Cottage Church Road Rich... ... Lukers in the County of Middlesex ... Austin Friars in the City of London ... of London Architect of the fifth part

Whereas by an Indenture dated the five... Richard Young Sarah Barrington and Elizab... of the then late dissolved Monastery or Priory... Friars London and upon which or parts of wh... and assigns thenceforth for the term of One ... released as hereinafter recited **And whilst** ... and made between the said Robert Stamper an... in the said term were assigned to the said Dan... redemption by the said Richard Young as therein ... hundred and two expressed to be made between ... and testament of the said Daniel Baker then dece... right of redemption then subsisting by virtue of... and by the same Indenture the said Richard Y... messuage in Austin Friars aforesaid with a piece... administrators and assigns thenceforth for the ter... Young to redeem the hereditaments comprised ... Three thousand one hundred and eighty pounds ... Assignments and operations of law ultimately t... and made between Benjamin Beakes Gundry an... Beakes Fra Gundry of the third part Thomas ... hereditaments comprised in the Indenture lastl... the said Thomas Alexander Roberts as to such p... thousand years and Five hundred years xxxx... hundred and ninety four and twenty nine J... hereditaments thereby conveyed as aforesaid exp... Richard Roberts his heirs and assigns upon trus... the said Thomas Alexander Roberts duly made... thereby (inter alia) gave and devised the heredi... house N° 18 Austin Friars London unto and ... assigns for her sole and separate use absolute... One thousand eight hundred and eighty eigh... December One thousand eight hundred and ...

by the said Thomas Gilbert Peckham Charles Hill Davy and Alexander Roberts the Executors therein named **And** ... sale to him for the sum of Twenty one thousand pounds of the hereditaments intended to be hereby conveyed but no... William Brass has agreed with the said William Capel Slaughter and William May to transfer to them the benefit of the ... the said William Brass the sum of Five thousand pounds making with the said sum of Twenty one thousand pounds ... sum of Twenty six thousand pounds **And whereas** the title dividing the property comprised in the term of One ... determined and it is not now possible to distinguish in which term the hereditaments expressed to be hereby conveyed are... have consented to concur in these presents in manner hereinafter expressed **Now this Indenture witnesseth** ... pounds to the said Florence Mary Rogers and of the sum of Five thousand pounds to the said William Brass respect... the said Florence Mary Rogers and William Brass do hereby respectively acknowledge they the said Thomas Gilbert Peckham ... direction of the said Florence Mary Rogers hereby convey and the said Florence Mary Rogers as beneficial Owner at the request of the sa... said William Capel Slaughter and William May **All that** piece or parcel of ground situated on the west side of Austin Friars in the ... Friars aforesaid but formerly known as N° 15 Winkworth Buildings all which hereditaments are delineated in the plan drawn on these p... open area other than those which are included in the hereinbefore recited Indenture of the twenty third January One thousand eigh... if any and the said William Capel Slaughter and William May their executors administrators and assigns as joint tenants as h... of April One thousand six hundred and ninety four for all the residue now to come of the said term and as to the remaining part the... time One thousand seven hundred and two **And this Indenture also witnesseth** that in pursuance of the said agree... Mary Rogers and at the request of the said William Brass do hereby convey and the said Florence Mary Rogers as Beneficial Ow... presents **All and singular** the hereditaments hereinbefore described and expressed to be hereby conveyed **To hold** unto and to the use... existing and affecting the same hereditaments in trust nevertheless for them the said William Capel Slaughter and William May their... of the said William Capel Slaughter and William May to produce on of the hereinbefore recited Indenture of the twenty third January... of the same **In witness** whereof the said parties to these presents have hereunto set their hands and seals the day and year be...

J.G. Peckham

C.H. Davy

A. Roberts

Florence M. Rogers

C. Brass

Wm Capel Slaughter

£130

NEW FOOTWAY

N° 24

N° 18   N° 17

AUSTIN FRIARS

AUSTIN FRIARS

N° 14